STAGE SOURCE BOOK
SETS
Gill Davies

STAGE SOURCE BOOK

SETS

Gill Davies

A & C Black ▪ London

First published 2004 by
A & C Black Publishers Limited
37 Soho Square
London W1D 3QZ

www.acblack.com

ISBN 0-7136-6586-6

Author
© **Gill Davies 2004**

© Playne Books Limited 2004

Stage Source Book SETS
was conceived, edited and designed by
Playne Books Limited
Chapel House
Trefin, Haverfordwest
Pembrokeshire SA62 5AU
United Kingdom

Research and editorial assistants
Vivienne Prior
Chris Skinner

Designers and illustrators
Richard Cotton
David Playne
Q2ASolutions

Typeset in Glypha

Playne Books Limited wish to thank
Jeff Parker and the
English Civil War Society
for the use of the photograph on page 52.

Pictures on pages 45, 46, 47, 48, 55, 57, 58, 59,
69, 72, 73, 85, 87, 90, 97, 98, 99 and 100 were
taken at the Museum of Welsh Life, Cardiff,
South Wales, United Kingdom

Pictures on pages 46, 56 and 58, were taken at
Llancaiach Fawr Manor, Rhymney Valley,
South Wales, United Kingdom

Printed in China

CIP catalogue records for this book are
available from the British Library and the
Library of Congress.

Introduction

A good all-round production is made possible only by attention to detail. From the director to the scenographer, it is concentration on those elements that matter and then drawing them all together that will give the play credence. The set designer's role is crucial but to analyse the needs of a particular set may require a good deal of research, especially if the period is historic. Many different sources will need to be tapped.

The aim of *Stage Source Book* **Sets** (and its companion volume *Stage Source Book* **Props**) is to simplify this gathering of information by bringing it all together into a single major resource. The book should eliminate the need for numerous visits to the library to gather in countless works of reference – and the subsequent deciphering of their contents – before beginning the design of a set that will look both pleasing and appropriate.

The book covers specific periods of time, from Ancient Egypt and the Romans to the 1990s, as well as specialist settings like forests, the seaside, international venues, trains and stations, snow scenes, fairgrounds and fairy tales. Numerous drawings and photographs capture the essence of each setting through the ages – with buildings that range from castles and palaces to humble farms and cottages – through architectural details such as doors and windows, interiors, and changing styles. Streets, shops and gardens are also illustrated. The emphasis varies from one period to another, as appropriate, and will sometimes include special features – such as Greek columns and French chateaux.

Obviously, while some fashionable settings are a pure reflection of their period, many houses mutate, sometimes through several centuries, to become a conglomerate mix. If historical accuracy is to be maintained, the main aim is to avoid styles and features not yet introduced!

With examples of plays from each category – plus useful background information on theatre development, architecture, major events and daily life – the book should prove a helpful source of information and inspiration. The great variety of play settings that grace the stages of the world has necessarily meant that some settings have escaped this volume but the contents cover a wide range of possibilities and I trust will, henceforth, prove an invaluable resource for the set designer.

Gill Davies

Contents

Sets for historical settings

8   Ancient Egypt
Age of the Pharoahs:
3000-30 BC

15   Ancient Greece
The birthplace of theatre:
780-323 BC

21   Ancient Rome
Imperial growth:
753 BC-324 AD

28   The Dark Ages
Invaders and raiders:
500-1000 AD

35   The Middle Ages
The Gothic period:
1000-1500

42   1500-1599
The age of Shakespeare

52   1600-1699
Puritanism versus opulence

65   1700-1799
The age of revolutions

81   1800-1899
Imperialism and industry

93   1900-2000
From bicycle to space travel

Exteriors

104   Woodland and forest

106   Field, moor and meadow

108   Stream, river and lakeland

110   Seaside and shore

112   Gardens

115   Mountain scenery

117   Clouds and sky

Contents

International Guidelines

120 The Far East

122 Africa

124 India

125 Australia

126 Northern/Central Europe

128 Paris

130 London

132 New York

134 Venice

136 Southern Europe

138 South America

Special areas

140 Wild West

142 Fairgrounds

143 Military scenes

144 Trains and stations

146 Shopping

148 Fairy tale and escapist

150 Snow scenes

151 Useful addresses
and suppliers

152 Periods and styles

154 British rulers

155 Prime Ministers
and Presidents

156 Bibliography
and further reading

157 Index

Ancient Egypt

Age of the Pharoahs: 3000-30 BC

Ancient Egypt had a rich and exotic lifestyle centuries before European civilisation flourished. The building of pyramids, in particular, has long been a source of fascination and inspiration. Both pyramid and obelisk had a strong influence on later architects all over the world, so much so that rich Europeans from Roman times onwards built themselves pyramid tombs.

Egyptians did not construct special venues for plays, but did perform religious and ritualistic pageants, satires, myths, and plays with symbolic dances. They used backdrops and musical instruments such as string harps, lyres, lutes, drums, flutes, clarinets, double pipes, trumpets, oboes, rattles, tambourines, bells and cymbals.

Plays set in Ancient Egypt:

Aida – Elton John and Leann Rimes

Aida – An opera by Verdi

Antony and Cleopatra – William Shakespeare

Caesar and Cleopatra – George Bernard Shaw

Firstborn – Christopher Fry

Joseph and His Amazing Technicolour Dreamcoat – Tim Rice and Andrew Lloyd Webber

And set in more recent times . . .
Death on the Nile – Agatha Christie

Lifestyle

Arts and crafts flourished under the patronage of the wealthy pharaohs. The Egyptians lived a relatively good life, and even slaves had plenty of food. Farmers tilled the fertile land along the Nile banks, where annual flooding enriched the soil and usually ensured ample crops to harvest. Just occasionally, as when Joseph helped the Pharoah, the Nile failed to rise and there was famine.

Building materials

Temples and tombs were built from stone – intended to last for eternity The houses of the living were made of mud brick. Ordinary people built their homes in villages while the pharaohs, and their entourage lived in vast palaces – still made of mud bricks.

Furnishings

The Egyptians slept in beds with linen sheets but had no pillows; they used headrests made of stone, ivory or wood. Small tables and stools were used. There were gilded and inlaid chairs, wig boxes, candlesticks, flower vases, gold and silver tableware and vessels made of alabaster, glass, faience and pottery. Wooden storage chests or caskets contained utensils or jewellery. There was highly skilled engraving and inlay work.

Wood was used for shelving and stone for column bases, steps, drainage systems and bathrooms. Brick walls were plastered and exteriors painted white. Interior walls and floors were often painted in vivid colours – as well as ceilings, doorways, windows and balconies. Decoration included stylized bullheads, leaping calves, plants, flowers, spiral vines, birds and feathers, gods and amulets, and bright gilded and glazed tiles. Craftsmen in royal workshops worked directly under the king's instructions, making fine furniture.

The importance of gold

Because it stayed new and bright, even if buried for years, gold was seen as a mystical material, associated with the sun and everlasting life. It was even believed that the gods were made of gold and so gold masks protected dead royalty. Gold was often given to neighbouring rulers to ensure a friendly relationship. A major source was Nubia, where gold ore was mined from mountains deep in the desert. The precious metal was carried back to the cities where royal goldsmiths made it into statues and jewellery. Gold could also be beaten into incredibly fine gold leaf and used for decoration.

Coffins and tombs

Many Old Kingdom coffins were vast. Some were shaped like houses or palaces because the Egyptians believed that the occupants would actually live there in the afterlife. Often, a pair of eyes was painted on the east side of a coffin so that the dead could see out.

Dynasties and pyramids

More than eighty pyramids of different shapes and sizes have been discovered in Egypt – most of them built as royal tombs. During the First Dynasty (3100–2890 BC), fine Royal tombs were being built near Abydos and Memphis.

In the Second Dynasty (2890–2686 BC), granite and slate statuary were popular. and there was greater use of stone in building plus fine metal, ivory, wood and faïence work.

In the Third Dynasty (2686-2613 BC), kings Zoser and Sanakht had large brick mastaba tombs built near Abydos. In 2650 , the first monumental stone building, the Step Pyramid in Saqqara, Memphis, had beautiful stone sculpture. Soon there was increasing boldness in the use of masonry blocks.

During the Fourth Dynasty, Memphis became the capital. Now timber was imported from Lebanon and copper was mined in Sinai. The Bent Pyramid of King Snefru was built at Dahshur. As monuments and written records became more numerous, the age of

Ancient Egypt

the great pyramid builders began, when royal tombs made of huge, stone blocks, smoothly faced, became the most important monuments for kings.

In Khafre's valley, vast monolithic pillars were hewn from Aswan granite. Between them were raised over twenty statues of the king. Meanwhile, the Sphinx was carved from an outcrop of rock. At Menkure, limestone and red granite pyramid temples were left unfinished.

While the very first pyramid (and first monumental stone building in the world) was the Step Pyramid at Saqqara, in later pyramids the stepped sides became smooth and the burial chamber moved from under the ground to inside the pyramid – which became part of a whole complex of buildings to protect dead royalty and help them on their journey to the afterlife. Beside the pyramid was a mortuary temple where offerings could be made to the king's spirit. The body was received by the priests and prepared for burial.

A covered passage or causeway led to a waterside valley temple, where royal mummies were carried to rest in a stone sarcophagus deep inside the pyramid. Finally the passages leading to the burial chamber were sealed with heavy stone slabs. Next to the king's pyramid were often smaller pyramids for royal wives, mothers and daughters.

The Great Pyramid at Giza, built 2570 BC, was one of the Seven Wonders of the Ancient World. Some 150 metres (450 ft) high, its sides of 2,000,000 stone blocks, each weighing some 2.5 tonnes, were covered with gleaming, polished white limestone. The tip was covered with gold to reflect the sun.

No more large stone pyramids were built after the 4th Dynasty. Late Old Kingdom pyramids were of rubble covered or 'cased' with stone, and soon fell into disrepair. Middle Kingdom pyramids were even more fragile, built over a mudbrick core, and most collapsed in ruins. During the New Kingdom, pharaohs began to be buried in rock-cut tombs in the Valley of the Kings.

Historic background

7000-3000 BC
Nomadic tribes settle on Nile banks.

3000 BC
King Narmer unites Upper Egypt (Aswan to Cairo) and Lower Egypt (Nile Delta) into one kingdom; Founding of state, administration, and calendar; invention of a script.

3100 BC
Hieroglyphic script used.

2900-2600 BC
Great Pyramids built at Giza.

2055 BC
Mentuhotep II gains control .

2000 BC
Karnak Temple begun; Egyptians control Nubia.

1600 BC
Ahmose unifies the country.

1500 BC
Hatshepsut is pharaoh.

1400 BC
Tutankhamun becomes pharaoh.

1274 BC
Ramesses II fights Battle of Kadesh.

1100 BC
Upper and Lower Egypt split.

945-730 BC
Libyans rule Egypt.

800-728 BC
Nubian king Piy conquers Egypt.

700-671 BC
Assyrians attack Egypt.

600-525 BC
Persians conquer Egypt.

400-332 BC
Alexander the Great conquers Egypt and founds Alexandria.

300 BC
Alexandrian Museum and Library.

289 BC
Ptolemy II builds lighthouse at Alexandria.

30 BC
Cleopatra VII, the last Egyptian queen, dies. Egypt a Roman province.

300 AD
Last use of hieroglyphic writing.

394-640 AD
Egypt ruled by Byzantine Constantinople.

600-642 AD
Egypt conquered by Arabs.

640 AD
Expulsion of Byzantines: Egypt a province of caliph kingdom.

900-969 AD
Cairo founded; casing blocks stripped off Giza pyramids.

Ancient Egypt **Pyramids and sphinx**

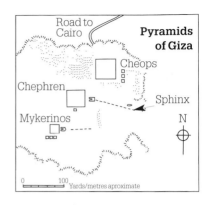

Pyramids of Giza

Road to Cairo

Cheops

Chephren

Sphinx

Mykerinos

N

0   100   Yards/metres aproximate

Pyramids and sphinx conjure up Ancient Egypt. Here also are depicted one of the huge Colossi of Memnon and a fine pharoah's head – many can be seen at temples such as Luxor or Abu Simbel

Temples today Ancient Egypt

Many fine temple buildings have survived the centuries in Egypt's dry heat

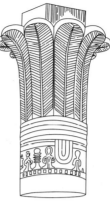

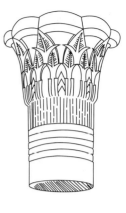

Columns
Composite, as at Esna

Volute, as at Philae

Hathor head, as at Philae

Palm, as at Edfu

Papyrus, as at Philae

Column with
bud capital at
Medinet
Habu

Osiris pillars, as at Thebes

Window at
Medinet Habu

Doorway, as at Philae

Detailed and
elaborate wall
paintings have
survived to vividly
depict Ancient
Egyptian life

Interior wall paintings and reliefs Ancient Egypt

Whether on wall paintings, cut into stone or as decoration on furniture or ceramics, people and gods are usually shown in profile

The lotus flower or bud might be painted naturally or used as a formal decorative motif, often in repeated patterns

In this instance wearing a composite crown, Thoth, the god of knowledge, is sometimes depicted with the head of an ibis. He can also take the form of a baboon

Royal boat: tall masts held an oblong, linen sail

Akhenaten (formerly Amenhotep) founded a capital in Tell el-Amarna and is presented with thick lips and narrow eyes

Papyrus: the word paper derives from this, which Egyptians made from the stems of tall papyrus reeds, sliced into strips, soaked and pressed together in a crisscross pattern to make a strong sheet

Bearded pharoah

After the Middle Kingdom, horses were used to pull chariots

Professional dancers were usually women who performed at rituals and funerals

Fowler: birds were hunted on the riverbank or in marshes

Man standing

Groseti kneeling

Ancient Greece

The birthplace of theatre: 780-323 BC

Ancient Greece saw the beginning of theatre and drama – as we understand it in the Western world. Here were philosophers, doctors, poets, scientists, astronomers and statesmen whose lifestyle allowed time for thought and argument, ideas and oratory. They sought perfection and balance in all things, including their architecture.

Ancient Greece

Greek theatres

Vast arenas had multiple entrances. They were set into the hillside where the natural contours provided fine acoustics and visibility. The theater of Dionysus in classical Athens was set on a slope below the Acropolis. At first, the audience stood or sat on the ground. Later, wooden or stone benches were raised on the hillside. Some theatres could hold up to 20,000 and became the prototypes for amphitheatres and sports arenas.

By the 5th century BC, a chorus and leader chanted lines. The chorus danced, sang, made sound effects and played musical instruments such as a lyre or pipe. They performed in the 'orchestra', not on a raised stage. The main actors portrayed mythical and historical characters, at first in an empty space but later in front of a rectangular structure where simple scene building represented settings. Actors changed costumes in dressing rooms set into the buildings of this backdrop façade. Stage machinery was sometimes used but scenes of war or violence usually took place offstage. Performances were in daylight – actors held up an oil lantern to show when it was night.

Masks denoted character, emotion or sex (only men performed). The concept of realistic characters only developed later as powerful playwrights emerged. In the 6th century BC, Thespis became both the first dramatist and first real actor and his name gave rise to the term thespian. Other playwrights included tragedians, Aeschylus and Sophocles, in whose works the role of the chorus grew as the focal point between characters. It was Euripides (480-406 BC) who introduced a naturalistic approach. Comedy playwrights included Aristophanes (448-380 BC) and Menander (342-292 BC) who used topical humour and satire. Tragedy reached a peak when Greek society was at its height; comedy became most popular during its decline.

Original Ancient Greek plays

The Bacchae – Euripides

Lysistrata – Aristophanies

Medea – Euripides

Oedipus at Colonus – Sophocles

Oedipus the King – Sophocles

The Trojan Women – Euripedes

More recent plays iunclde:

Goodbye Iphigenia – George MacEwan Green

Love of the Nightingale – Timberlake Wertenbaker

A Phoenix too Frequent – Christopher Fry

Rape of the Belt – Benn W Levy

Troilus and Cressida – William Shakespeare

Life at home

Most Greek houses were built only with bricks with the addition of some mud. In the towns the houses were uusually small, but in the country larger villas might be created. Whether in town or rural areas, there was sparse furniture.

In the 6th and 5th century BC, Greek houses, built of stone, wood, or clay bricks, consisted of two or three rooms, built around an open air courtyard. Larger homes sometimes had a kitchen, a room for bathing, a dining room for the men of the houshold and their guests and a woman's sitting area.

Small windows restricted the sun indoors to keep rooms cool while overhanging roofs created shady areas in the central courtyards.

The men of the household were treated with great respect and relaxed on couches, to be fed and entertained by slaves. Usually the women and children ate and slept in another room. Furniture was sparse but elegant

Courtyards

Greek women were allowed to leave their homes for only brief excursions and so their main opportunity to enjoy the open air was in the privacy of their courtyard where they could relax, converse, and sew. The ancient Greeks believed a pale complexion was a sign of beauty so on sunny days, the women probably sheltered under a covered area. In general, the courtyard was an important area for Greek family life, a place where they gathered to listen to stories and fables – and to eat. The cooking equipment was small and light and so was mobile enough to be set up in the courtyard when required.

Greek civilisation

The Greeks built great cities with fine buildings and were also excellent boat builders – which helped their civilisation to spread to Italy and the Eastern Mediterranean. The city centered around the agora (market place) where there were public buldings including temples and law courts, as well as shops. Athens was a vast rich city and the centre of

Greek culture but was dusty and had poor water supplies. Houses were used only for eating and sleeping. The concentration was on the fine temples and public buildings.

Greek architecture

Buildings were constructed with bricks made from mud, stone, and wood. Marble and limestone were introduced by the end of the 7th century BC and by the next century, terracotta baked tiles were being used for roofing and gables. Multicoloured seaside pebbles were implemented to create mosaics.

Architecture was dominated by religion and so the temples were the most beautiful buildings – their simple elegancy a celebration of civic power and pride. They were relatively small but had fine tall entrance doors. Windows were rare and some temples may have been open to the sky. Statue chambers (accessible only to priests) contained a god's sacred image. Temples were usually raised on a natural hill

The Athenians, in particular, had access to excellent marble quarries. The strength of marble allowed it to support very heavy loads and so it was used for the columns. The Greeks adjusted the number of columns across the ends of a building in relation to those down the sides – to keep a pleasing balance.

In the 5th century BC, Greece was still an assortment of independent city-states but in 338 BC, Philip II of Macedon drew them all together into a single, vast empire and launched the Hellenistic Age. Then his son, Alexander the Great, conquered Egypt, Mesopotamia, Iran, and parts of India so Greek architecture suddenly became part of the powerful Hellenic empire as monumental cities rose with palaces and public halls, libraries, colonnaded avenues, squares and plazas, and vast tombs.

Columns were constructed in a raw fashion first before the final product was produced. The three types of columns are Doric, Ionic, and Corinthian. All have three separate parts to their structure – the base, shaft, and capital, although in Doric columns, the base is all one piece as is the capital.

Doric columns were used in mainland Greece and the colonies in southern Italy and Sicily. The Ionic style was thinner and more elegant with capitals decorated with a scroll-like design used in eastern Greece and the islands. The Corinthian style was rare in the Greek world, but often appeared on Roman temples. The capitals were very elaborate and decorated with acanthus leaves.

Historic background

780 - 560 BC
Greek colonies set up.

776 BC
First Olympiad.

753 BC
Legend claims Rome founded.

621 BC
Athens ruled by an oligarchy. Nobleman, Draco, appointed to create a code of laws, establishing death as punishment for all crimes.

580-489 BC
Pythagoras.

663 BC
Assyrian Empire peaks.

660 BC
Empire of Japan begins.

525 BC
Persians conquer Egypt.

509 BC
Roman Republic founded.

508 BC
Athenian democracy established.

499 BC
Greek city states revolt in Asia Minor against Persian rule.

490 BC
Greeks defeat Persians at Marathon.

460-370 BC
Hippocrates, physician, is 'father' of medicine.

431-404 BC
Peloponnesian War between Athens and Sparta.

429-347 BC
Plato

399 BC
Death of Socrates.

395 - 387 BC
Corinthian War.

390 BC
Celts sack Rome.

332 BC
Alexander the Great conquers Egypt.

323 BC
Death of Alexander the Great.

300 BC
Greek mathematician Euclid sets out principals of geometry.

Parthenon Ancient Greece

The Parthenon, topping the Aceropolis in Athens, is built in the Doric order. It is made of pentelic marble and surrounded by free-standing columns

Built 447-438 BC and dedicated to Athena Parthenos, patron goddess of Athens, it remains an international symbol of Ancient Greek civilization

Ancient Greece **Temples as they are today**

Temple at Delphi

Figures of caryatids act as columns and grace the Erechtheion, Athens

Temple of Zeus, Athens

Doric   Ionic   Corinthian

Canephora (maidens bearing baskets) make decorative columns

Caryatid, priestess of Artemis

Doric capital

Ionic capital

Corinthian capital

Theatres, reliefs and sculptures Ancient Greece

Theatres were buit into the natural contours of the hillside and had superb acoustics

Bulls at the Delos sanctuary

Detail of the Parthenon frieze, Athens

Statues, three-dimensional relief carvings of figures and busts (especially of philosophers and poets) are all popular art forms in Classical Greece and the Hellenistic period

Ancient Rome

Imperial Growth: 753 BC-324 AD

The Empire grew from its small city origins over 1,000 years to dominate much of the known world. Having initially adopted many Greek traditions, the Romans created a practical society and spread their knowledge and technology through a vast territory – making fine structures, cities served by aqueducts and an intricate network of roads, and finally adopting Christianity.

Ancient Rome

Theatre in Ancient Rome

By 400 BC, painting depicted sets. In time, raised stages arrived with temporary narrow wooden platforms about 30 metres (100 ft) long and a stage house with openings for entrances. Later this was decorated with columns, statues, niches, and porticoes, and covered by a roof. Scenery was described as tragic (palatial columns), comic (homely dwellings), or satyric (landscape). The first permanent stone theatre was built by Pompeius in 55-52 BC. A front curtain dropped into a slot at the beginning of a performance and was raised at the end. Roman actors wore contemporary garments and masks depicting multiple roles.

The Colosseum held 45,000 spectators. Many amphitheatres were of concrete, faced with stone. The Circus Maximus, used for chariot racing and made famous in *Ben Hur*, could seat 250,000. Gladiator fights, chariot races, music, dance, boxing, and battles were staged – sometimes against wild animals. Amphitheatres could be flooded for mock battles at sea or to show victims being fed to hungry crocodiles.

By AD 354, there was entertainment on over 100 festival days per year. Strolling players performed too, on simple timber platforms raised on posts. As Christianity spread, bawdier playacting became sinful in the eyes of the Church. Moreover, the arena was associated with martyrdom and pagan rituals. Roman theatre declined as the Empire expanded and the last recorded performance in Rome was in 533 AD. Plays by Plautus, Terence, and Seneca survive today. Terence (190-159 BC) introduced the subplot, and Plautus (c.250-184 BC) greater humour. Soon outrageous farce and slapstick were popular, although serious plays were still recited.

Plays about the Romans include:

Antony and Cleopatra – William Shakespeare

Britannicus – Racine

Caesar and Cleopatra – George Bernard Shaw

Coriolanus – William Shakespeare

A Funny Thing Happened on the Way to the Forum – Stephen Sondheim, Burt Shevelove and Larry Gelbart

Julius Caesar – William Shakespeare

The Roman Actor – Philip Massinger

Trial of Lucullus – Bertolt Brecht

Cities and towns

2,000 years ago, Rome was busy, crowded and noisy. In narrow streets lined with shops, wagons and covered litters thronged, soldiers marched, shoppers and workers hurried along and boys scurried to and from school. The city boasted theatres, baths, granaries, statues and memorials, libraries, fine temples and beautiful public buildings. In the Forum, the main marketplace in every Roman city, court sessions were held, and Senate orators argued, it was a business centre for banking and trade, as well as the place for festivals and religious ceremony.

Baths

Most public baths allotted separate time for men and women but the time allotted to females was less. Public baths were very popular and Romans used them at least once a day. The baths had cold and hot pools (basement furnaces heated the water), towels, steam rooms, saunas, exercise rooms, and hair cutting salons – all with slaves in attendance. They incorporated reading rooms, libraries, gardens and shops. At one time, there were as many as 900 public baths in Rome. Small ones held about 300 people, and the larger ones some 1600. Some Roman hospitals had their own bathhouses.

Homes

Poor folk lived in crowded shabby tenements, often above or behind shops. Fires were common because many generations crowded into one room to live and cook, without running water (they use public latrines) and many of the flats were made of wood.

Successful tradesmen often lived over the store in relatively spacious rooms. The rich lived in gracious homes. The entrance atrium was the centre of upper class family life. Their homes were generally of brick with red tile roofs, and, like the Greek villas, had rooms arranged around a central courtyard with a covered walk (peristyle) around this. They grew their favourite roses, irises, marigiolds, delphiniums and peonies.

The windows and balconies faced the courtyard, not the street. There were paintings on the walls and beautiful mosaics on the floor but very little furniture. Most Romans had a shrine in their home, which might be relatively small or a grand, separate room to honour the household god. Wealthy, Roman single-storey villas included bedrooms, office, kitchen, dining-living room, garden, temple, atrium, toilet, and private bath. Their were lit with oil lamps. Slaves kept the furnaces burning in the bath houses, cooked, cleaned, sewed, and worked in the garden. Often, the rich also owned farms and country estates, usually run by reliable slaves. Here the family could escape from the dust and turmoil of the city.

Furnishings

In early times, the dining table was in the atrium and the family sat on stools as children waited on their parents along with the slaves. Later, a separate dining room was used and couches replaced benches or stools. Oil lamps and occasionally candles lit the rooms at night and they were heated with portable braziers.

Roads, building and aqueducts

The Romans built thousands of miles of roads, linking every part of the Empire. The Colosseum was built of concrete (this was an ancient Roman invention) faced with stone, as were most amphitheaters. Concrete served to build the dome of the Pantheon temple – still one of the largest single-span domes in the world. They also used concrete to build the underwater port at Caesarea in Israel.

Aqueducts supplied cities with adequate fresh water. Massive aqueducts and supply lines were constructed, sometimes across valleys on arches – or, more commonly, through underground conduits of clay or wood, covered or encrusted with stone. The pipes inside the conduits were made of lead, mostly mined in Spain. As the Empire spread, pipeline had to be transported further and further afield. Since the ancient Romans didn't use pumps, aqueducts had to be built at a relatively constant gradient for many miles to ensure continuous supply.

Forts and ports

Roman soldiers were stationed in forts – usually wooden structures but later built (or rebuilt) in stone. Behind the strong fort gates and high walls were the barracks, baths, granary, stables, the commander's house, offices and archives, storerooms, strongrooms, prison and hospital – in a formal, regular lay-out that was similar whatever the location.

Ports were established across the empire and vast amounts of food, barrels of beer, wine and exotic goods (silk, jewels, spices and perfumes) travelled by sea in the safer summer months, in merchant ships with a single, large, square sail and a smaller sail for steering at the front. Galleys patrolled the sea to deter pirates, and lighthouses, with permanent fires burning, were set at harbour entrances. Flat-bottomed barges carried goods further up river.

Historic background

509 BC
Roman Republic founded.

490 BC
Battle of Marathon.

395 - 387 BC
Corinthian War.

370 BC
1st Roman roads built.

356-323 BC
Wars of Alexander the Great.

264-146 BC
Punic Wars.

221 BC
Great Wall of China built.

215 BC
Archimedes discovers gravity.

168 BC
Rome conquers Macedonia.

144 BC
Aqueducts bring Rome water.

58-43 BC
Caesar conquers Gaul and Britain.

44 BC
Caesar assassinated.

25 AD
Han Dynasty founded.

30 AD
Christ crucified.

54 AD
Claudius murdered; Nero rules.

64 AD
Rome nearly destroyed in fire.

79 AD
Vesuvius destroys Pompeii.

80-404 AD
Colosseum used for gladiator games.

122 AD
Hadrian's Wall built.

235-284 AD
Roman civil wars.

317 AD
Tartar warriors break through Great Wall of China.

320 AD
Gupta Empire: golden age of Indian culture.

330 -335 AD
Emperor Constantine I creates new capital at Constantinople and makes Christianity legal.

Rome Colosseum Ancient Rome

Colosseum in Rome was raised by Vespasian in AD 80 and was used for glatiator events, hunts and mock battles until 404AD. The arena held some 55,000 spectators; it could be flooded for staging naval battles – or for fights with crocodiles

Aqueducts supplied cities with water. Roman engineers used vast cranes and pulleys and gangs of slaves to quarry the stone and then build these massive water systems

The first permanent stone theatre was built by Pompeius in 55-52 BC. In time Roman theatres had raised stages and a 'stage house' with openings for entrances

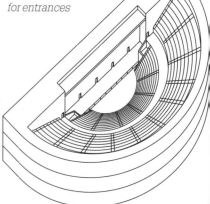

Ancient Rome **Mosaics, carvings, meal in a villa**

Roman lettering at Arycanda, Turkey

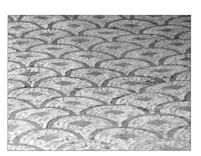

Good food was an important element of life and the rich had elaborate dinner parties

Mosaic decorated the floors of homes and public buildings. These could take the form of repeated patterns or might be a complete image surrounded by a border

Ephesus library, Rome Forum Ancient Rome

Library at ancient Ionian city of Ephesus in today's Turkey

Temple of Saturn, the Forum, Rome

Ceremonial triumphal arches commemorated victories all over the empire, and were often decorated with battle scenes

Row of Corinthian columns.

The Forum in Rome, glimpsed through the Arch of Septimius Severus

Ionic columns

Pediment with relief figures of soldiers in battle

At the Pantheon in Rome (AD120-24), a Corinthian portico leads to a massive rotunda: this is one of the best preserved ancient buildings in the city

Roman decorative details included carved figures and patterned reliefs. Pillar capitals, in particular, were often richly carved

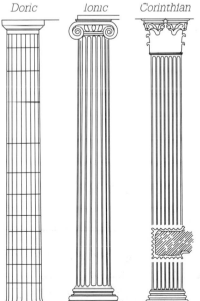

Doric   Ionic   Corinthian

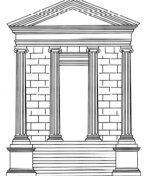

Elevation and side elevation of the Temple of Fortuna Virilis in Rome

Roman towns were protected by strong walls – with heavy gatehouses at the entrances. Within were many shops, homes and offices, the market place and forum, taverns, fine public buildings, theatres, amphitheatres, racecourses and baths. Aqueducts brought water into the towns but only the rich had this pumped directly into their homes. Most used the water in public fountains and had to visit multi-seated public latrines connected to underground sewers.

The buildings were generally of brick and concrete with expensive stone used only for the more important buildings. Roof tiles were of moulded clay, baked in kilns.

The Romans perfected the art of building domes. In peacetime, the army helped to plan and build towns while slaves worked as labourers.

The Dark Ages

Invaders and raiders: 500-1000 AD

The Roman influence was gone: Christianity diminished temporarily but then spread in Wales and Ireland (especially through Saint Patrick) and in Scotland. Monasteries sprang up but by the end of the 8th century, Vikings began their raids and plunder. Alfred the Great (871-899) defended England, established a navy, laws, and a written English language but the Danes returned after he died and King Ethelred paid them Danegeld.

Influences on theatre

The Roman Empire had fallen. As the centuries passed, Christianity recovered and gradually spread to dominate much of the Western world. Drama was considered by the Church to be a corrupt influence, so theatre development was repressed. However, roving bands of street players, jugglers, acrobats and animal trainers retained some traditions and stock characters. In time, performances of Biblical stories were allowed in churches. A stage was erected near the altar, with temporary platforms for the more distant scenes. In time, many stages or platforms were used for different scenes – called 'mansions'. Easter and Nativity characters were played by priests, in productions that grew more elaborate. Performances moved from inside the church to just outside and, then into the marketplace where they developed into the popular entertainment of medieval times.

Plays set in the Dark Ages:

Boy with a Cart – Christopher Fry

Camelot – Frederick Loewe and Alan Jay Lerner

Götterdämmerung – Richard Wagner

The Rhinegold – Richard Wagner

Siegfried – Richard Wagner

Tales of King Arthur – John Chambers

Thor, with Angels – Christopher Fry

The Valkyrie – Richard Wagner

Lifestyle

As Barbarian Goths, Vandals, and Huns swept through Europe, destroying buildings and works of art. pagan Anglo-Saxons invaded Britain in the 5-7th centuries. There were very few schools so education diminished and only in monasteries did the arts survive. War leader kings or chiefs and barbaric tribes dominated small enclaves. Slavery was a huge commercial enterprise and many Celtic Britons became slaves. Wealthier rulers lived on estates or large farmsteads. Lavish feasts and entertainment took place in their great rectangular halls, decorated with wall hangings.

The Vikings

By the end of the 9th century, the Danes had settled in East Anglia and Northumberland where they founded several small kingdoms in an area called Danelagen. As Viking fleets continued to raid for food and slaves, the English raised strongholds in the south to defend their territory. The Vikings were great warriors, both on land and at sea, and colonised much of the northern world. They attacked Britain's holy places, slaughtered monks and stole many treasures From the end of the 700s, they made voyages of discovery and seasonal raids, and then returned home to farm. Their settlements, burials and sagas reveal a fascinating culture.

Poor people lived in round, wooden huts with thatched or turfed roofs. With wattle and daub walls, they were highly flammable. Even nobles and officials lived in wooden halls, albeit larger. A few churches and monasteries were of stone.

Churches and monasteries

A few stone monasteries and churches survived the warfare, invasion and plunder, and date from either 600-725 or 900-1050. The Synod of Whitby in 664 encouraged Roman Christian observance and northern churches absorbed basilican styles and had plain walls, plus a rounded chancel in the east. Some retained Celtic origins, with tall naves, no aisle and a rectangular chancel. Most early Saxon churches were small and simple with the nave divided from a rectangular chancel by a narrow arch. Few large churches from 900 to 1050 survived and many monasteries were rebuilt in Norman times so little Saxon work remains visible.

Doors and window openings were simple, with few decorative elements. Windows were low triangles or narrow slit openings with a simple rounded top. Larger openings were often supported on short pillars of plain stone or simple balusters. The chancel and nave were small, rectangular enclosures, almost cut off from each other.

The tower was often the only part of a Saxon church to survive. Used as a defensive structure for village or town, it provided a lookout point, with high rooms, reached by a ladder that could be drawn up if danger threatened. Stonework in exterior walls often incorporated long strips of vertical stone, usually in a simple criss-cross pattern. At the corners, alternate horizontal and vertical stones might be used.

Saxon crosses were often used to mark points where paths intersected, although they later became a place for religious observance. Crosses may have been raised at sites regarded as sacred in earlier pagan worship. Later on, a churches might be built on the site. Circle crosses can be found in places with strong Celtic traditions, such as Wales and Ireland. The arms of the cross extend just to, or just beyond, a circle of protective stone.

The Dark Ages

Designs incised on the surface of crosses show elements of both Christian and pagan worship and include Biblical figures, and intricate scrolls of leaves and vines.

Domestic architecture

Nobles' halls were simple, with a central fire and a hole in the roof to let out the smoke. Generally there was only one floor and one room. Most were square or rectangular, with the occasional round house. A sunken plank floor was suspended over a shallow pit – probably filled with straw for insulation. In towns, the pits were sometimes 3 metres (9 ft) deep, suggesting they were used as a storage or work area.

Simple post framing was common, with heavy posts sunk into the ground to support the roof. The space between the posts was filled in with wattle and daub, or planks. Floors were packed earth, or sometimes planks. Cruck framing (two large timbers bent together to form a peak) was used, but was more common in Norman times. Thatch was used for roofing, or sometimes turf and wooden shingles. Windows were rare and were covered with thin animal skins to allow light to penetrate. There may have been occasional glazing in the late Saxon period.

Anglo-Saxon towns

Populations ranged from 500 in St. Albans to 5,000 in York. Most travellers followed main trade routes that traced old Roman roads. Alfred the Great encouraged the formation of fortified towns, located primarily along the coast and the borders of his lands. In exchange for free plots of land, settlers provided a defence force and towns become centres of commerce and local government.

Edward the Elder continued this policy; he and his sister built a double row of burhs (towns) along the old Roman road of Watling Street, which marked the border of the Danelaw running from the Mersey to Essex. Usually set at major road junctions, the towns had a regular grid pattern of streets. Old Roman towns already had basic fortifications in place and perimeter walls or earthwork defences could easily be repaired and strengthened. New streets ran alongside houses raised on Roman street foundations. Other Saxon burhs were set on entirely new sites, built on promontories of land, with a simple ditch and bank defence.

Historic background

455
Anglo Saxons attack England.

455
Vandals sack Rome.

503 - 557
Persian-Roman Wars.

516
The historical figure of Arthur, a military leader of the Britons, battles against the Saxons (and in 537).

565
Justinian the Great dies after 38 years as ruler of Byzantine Empire.

598
Pope Gregory's truce ensures Rome's independence.

604
Prince Shotoku reforms Japan.

618
T'ang Dynasty founded.

622
Mohammed flees to Medina.

635
Persians defeated by Arabs.

637-678
Arab forces seize Jerusalem, conquer Egypt.and take Constantinople.

700
Chinese invent gunpowder.

711-718
Conquest of Spain by Muslims.

794 (-1185)
Kyoto period in Japan.

800
Coronation of Charlemagne.

843
Kingdom of Franks divides into three.

850
Mayan civilisation collapses.

851
Vikings sack London.

862
Vikings found Russia.

867
Basil founds Macedonian Dynasty.

871-899
Alfred the Great, King of Wessex. He will win victory over Danes in 878.

962
Otto I crowned Holy Roman Emperor.

982
Eric the Red visits Greenland.

1000
Vikings reach America.

The Dark Ages Istanbul and Jerusalem

Dome of Aghia Sofia, Istanbul, a Christian church raised in 532-7 by Justinian on the site of a church built by Constantine. It was converted into a mosque in 1453

Early Christian icon, painted in Aghia Sofia, Istanbul

Dome of the Rock built in Jerusalem 685-91 by Caliph Omar

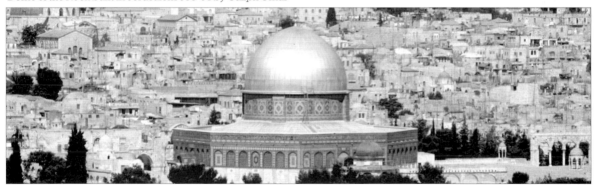

Celtic Britons and Irish The Dark Ages

Dark Age Celtic Britons lived in round huts in hill strongholds and fortified enclosures, similar to those of the Iron Age

Typical hut circle

Oratory of Gallerus, Ireland, c. 700 AD

The Book of Kells, c. 800 AD

Typical stone church

Celtic cross

Ogham stone

Life in the longhouse or hall: interiors and exteriors

The rural farming community was based around the longhouse or the lord's hall and was, in peacetime, dominated by seasonal demands and family needs

The Vikings The Dark Ages

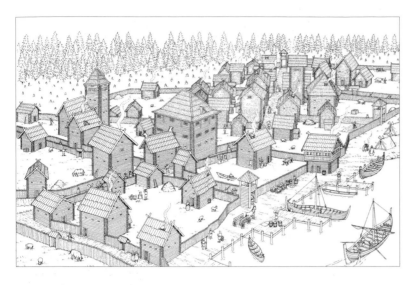

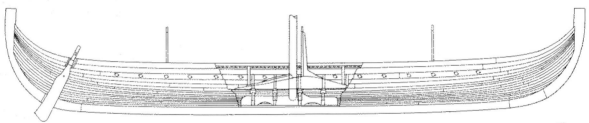

The Viking longship was narrow with a high prow, often serpentine and richly carved. Fast, lightweight and with a shallow draught, these were ideal vessels for navigating the narrow fjords, for making raids upriver and for landing on sandy beaches. The Atlantic ships had high sides and could accommodate over 30 pairs of oars. Trading ships would be loaded with chests and piles of cargo. It took the Danes only 13 years to conquer one third of England.

Many lived in fear of Viking raids as these fierce warriors sought new land, often across uncharted seas

Viking Runes
inscribed on a
standing stone

The Middle Ages

The Gothic Period: 1000-1500

This sweeping period is launched with the
Norman Conquest and ends as Tudor rule begins.
The medieval world has been much romanticized
with visions of Camelot, knights, castles and fairy
tale scenarios – but this was also a time of
turbulent warfare and hard-won thrones, the
Crusades and the Black Death.

Middle Ages

Influences on theatre

For a long time playacting had been regarded as ungodly by the Church so only plays with a religious theme were allowed. It is ironic that the Church, which had closed theatres, now became the mainspring of keeping drama alive, using drama to demonstate seasonal Biblical stories. At first, roles were played by priests in the sanctuary of the church but as performances grew more elaborate they moved outside to the church steps and thence to the marketplace.

Soon travelling players, minstrels, masked bands and mummers depicted Christian ideals, and legends such as St George killing the dragon. Scripts became more complex, mixing serious religious subjects with boisterous farce. Fixed stages began to use elaborate machinery with pulleys and ropes for special effects like moving clouds. Actors disappeared through trapdoors, while fire and smoke created the Mouth of Hell. While fixed stages were common in Europe, movable stages were used in England and Spain. Different scenes or stories were housed on carts and wheeled around to various venues or groups of spectators.

The three types of medieval plays were: cycles (mystery plays dramatizing biblical material in several short scenes; miracle plays depicting scenes from the lives of saints and martyrs; morality plays exploring the conflict between Vice and Virtue. These flourished in the mid-15th century and opened the door for secular Renaissance drama, further encouraged by the growth of towns and more stable governments.

From the the 1200s, travelling entertainers had wandered all over Europe, carrying everything with them on loaded wagons. Now there were also minstrels, singers, comedians, jugglers, acrobats, and troubadours. Itinerant actors were often regarded as vagabonds but plays were also staged by members of local guilds . When artisan guilds took charge of performances the local industry could be promoted!

Titles set in the Middle Ages:

Many plays by Shakespeare include *Henry V and Richard III*

Abelard and Heloise – Ronald Millar

Becket or the Honour of God – Jean Anouilh

Camelot – A J Lerner and F Loewe

Canterbury Tales – Chaucer; modernized by Phil Woods

Curtmantle – Christopher Fry

Francis – Julian Mitchell

Lady's not for Burning – Christopher Fry

Lark – Jean Anouilh, translated by Christopher Fry

The Lion in Winter – James Goldman

Richard of Bordeaux – Gordon Daviot

Robin Hood – several versions

Two planks and a passion – Anthony Minghella

Castles

The first castles were built only by the king or with his approval. A motte and bailey castle was raised on top of a large mound and surrounded by a deep ditch, beyond which lay the bailey, with stables, storehouses, bakeries, kitchens, cottages, and soldiers' quarters. A surrounding wooden palisade – and outer ditch, sometimes filled with water – gave protection. Most castles were rebuilt in the early and mid-12th century as stone keeps. Now thick, high walls enclosed a circular area. Bedrooms, garderobes and passages were created inside the thick walls. The keep basement was used for storage – or dungeons. Soldiers and servants lived on the ground floor. On the first floor, the Great Hall was a communal living area. The lord and his family resided on the second floor and there was often a chapel here. The roof housed kitchens and ovens (used for cooking or to heat up oil, water or burning brands to deter enemies). An outer defensive wall surrounded the keep. The gatehouse had an iron and wood portcullis, worked by chains.

Edwardian castles raised in the mid-1200s had concentric rings of walls, one inside the other, with towers all along these. A central open courtyard was surrounded by domestic buildings. The outer wall was ringed by a moat with a drawbridge. However, in the 14th century, the invention of cannons made castles less easy to defend. Large castles became palaces, and smaller ones fortified manor houses. Meals were held in the Great Hall, lit by candles and draped with tapestries. The lord's table was raised on a dais at one end. Travelling musicians played in a gallery, overlooking the hall, and would spread news and gossip as well as songs.

Manor houses

By the 13th century the fortified manor house was built in brick or stone, with a timber roof. The fire was still open and the hall was home to servants and retainers, but now the solar was added – a private room for the lord and his family on the first floor. A kitchen area, at first separated from the hall by wooden screens, in time became a totally separate room. The main entrance still might include moat, gatehouse and drawbridge.

In the 1300s, a buttery appeared between kitchen and hall, with a guest room above. There were elaborate porches, rooms with separate roofs, several storeys with private bedrooms, reception and family areas – and bricks. Now comfort dominated defence. Bridges replaced drawbridges over the moat and elaborate gatehouses made grand entrances.

Towns

Serfs often ran away to the towns; if they could stay for a year and a day they became free townsmen. As the Black Death diminished, populations swelled and burgeoning towns led to increased trade. Now merchant guilds controlled local government and regulated prices, quality and business practice. Each guild looked after the health, welfare and families of its members. Meanwhile, craft guilds also regulated working hours, conditions and the quality of work. Parents paid a fee to place a boy as an apprentice. He received food, clothes, and training for 2-7 years, after which he became a journeyman, paid by the day. After several more years, with the approval of the guild and submission of a 'master-piece', a journeyman might become a master craftsman and own his own shop.

In the narrow town streets, open drain channels ran along the sides or down the centre. Muck heaps spread out from stables. People threw out dirty water and emptied chamber pots from windows. Dyers' vats also emptied into the street and pigs were let out to forage.

Houses were half-timbered, or wattle and daub, whitewashed with lime, with roofs of reeds, rushes and straw. Fire was a constant threat in the closely packed wooden buildings. Morning was the time for noisy, raucous markets. As trade slowed, most shops closed by 3pm. A few kept open until dusk but barbers and blacksmiths were busy until the curfew bell sounded at 8 or 9 pm.

Historical Background

1066
Norman Conquest.

1095-1270
The Crusades.

1187
Muslims conquer Jerusalem.

1206
Genghis Khan founds Mongol Empire.

1215
Magna Carta in England.

1217
French-English wars.

1271-75
Marco Polo visits China.

1298
Scots rebel against English.

1314-17
Great European famine.

1326
Ottoman Empire founded.

1337-1453
Hundred Years War.

1346
Cannons first used as field weapons.

1347-53
The Black Death.

1364
Ming Dynasty founded.

1381
Peasants Revolt in England.

1429
Joan of Arc frees Orleans.

1438-1553
Inca dynasty in Peru.

1450
Printing press invented.

1452-1519
Leonardo da Vinci.

1453
Byzantine Empire ends as Constantinople falls to Turks.

1455–1485
Wars of the Roses.

1475-1564
Michelangelo.

1480
Spanish Inquisition.

1485
Tudor dynasty in England begins.

1492
Columbus sails to find New World.

Medieval settings The Middle Ages

1400s battle tent

Powerful lion statue guards a castle courtyard

Mummers' play

A king's or bishop's throne

Jousting tournament

Medieval street scene

Heraldic banner

Notre Dame in Paris, built c. 1163-1250, has superb flying buttresses, stained glass windows and gargoyles

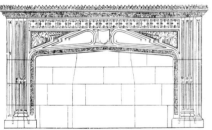

Mantelpiece and fire surround (1400s); as in a castle or fortified manor house

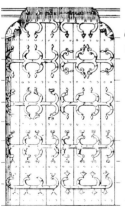

Stout decorated defensive doors

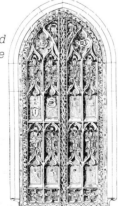

St Mark's, Venice

Churches

In the early Norman era, Romanesque architecture had barrel vaults, round arches, thick piers, and few windows. Church design was stark and solid, but walls were hung with tapestries or richly painted. The spacious, graceful Gothic style began in 12th century France – with pointed arches, ribbed vaults, slender clusters of columns, high spires and windows with coloured glass in a tracery of stonework.

Early English (1200-1275) had pointed lancet windows, slender towers topped with spires, and piers with narrow, clustered shafts. Decorated Gothic (1275-1375) brought fanciful tracery and ornamentation and wider windows – made possible by the new flying buttress. Stone decoration was rich and window glass colourful.

Finally, the Perpendicular period (1375-1530) had strong vertical lines in window tracery and wall panelling, and elaborate fan-shaped vaulting. Towers were elaborately decorated and pinnacled, vast windows had intricate stonework, and interiors were spacious.

500 years of change The Middle Ages

Norman or Romanesque 1066 - 1200

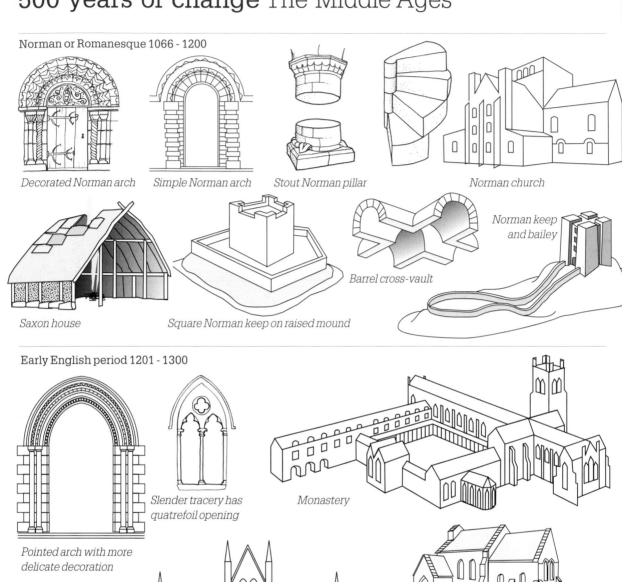

Decorated Norman arch

Simple Norman arch

Stout Norman pillar

Norman church

Norman keep and bailey

Saxon house

Square Norman keep on raised mound

Barrel cross-vault

Early English period 1201 - 1300

Slender tracery has quatrefoil opening

Monastery

Pointed arch with more delicate decoration

From church to castle to fortified manor house, throughout the Gothic period, buildings were sturdy and defensive but also highly decorative. French Gothic cathedrals were more flamboyant than their English counterparts with higher naves and flying buttresses.

Early English parish church

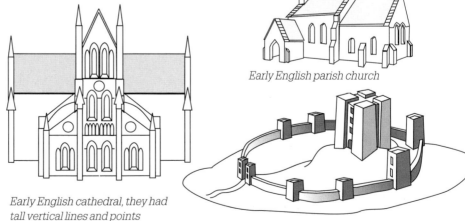

Early English cathedral, they had tall vertical lines and points

Castle from 1200s with keep, gatehouse and bailey

The Middle Ages **500 years of change**

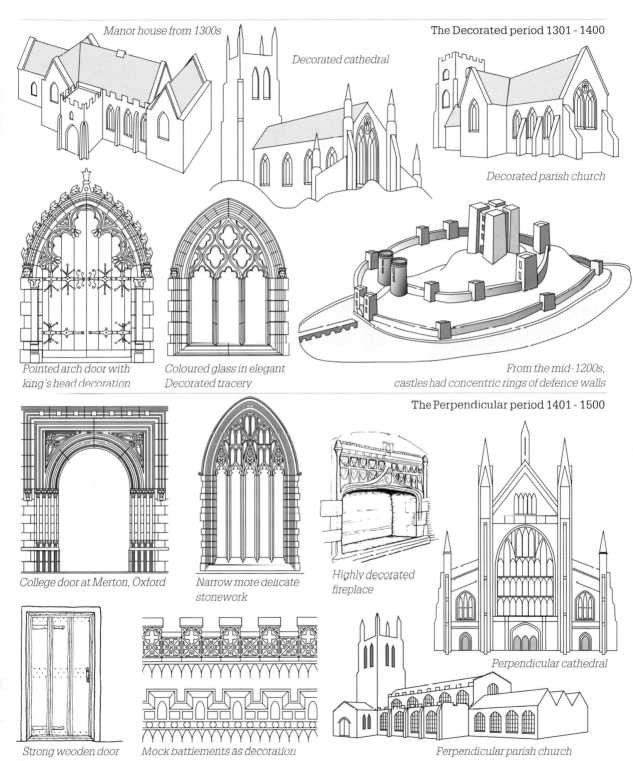

Manor house from 1300s

Decorated cathedral

Decorated parish church

Pointed arch door with king's head decoration

Coloured glass in elegant Decorated tracery

From the mid-1200s, castles had concentric rings of defence walls

The Perpendicular period 1401 - 1500

College door at Merton, Oxford

Narrow more delicate stonework

Highly decorated fireplace

Perpendicular cathedral

Strong wooden door

Mock battlements as decoration

Perpendicular parish church

1500-1599

The age of Shakespeare

From the Tudors to Elizabeth I in England, through Shakespeare's plays and and the Italian Renaissance, this was a time of great splendour, and advances in science, art and world exploration. It witnessed the great works of Michelangelo, Copernicus, Galileo and Da Vinci, the discoveries of Magellan, Drake and Cortes, the opening up of the Americas – and Ivan the Terrible in Russia.

Influences on theatre

Travelling groups used a simple platform, painted backcloth and trap doors. Now theatre separated from religion and commedia dell'arte became hugely popular, with its knockabout humour and ribald jokes. Productions became more lavish and permanent theatres were soon be built with raked stages.

The Italians used lenses, silk filters and liquids in front of candles to colour the stage. Auditoriums were darkened to make lit stages appear brighter. Classic Roman plays were revived and proscenium stage emerged. In England, enclosed inn courtyards had thrust stages: the audience were on three sides interacting with the performers. London's Globe had a circular auditorium with galleries around a thrust stage. The underside of its protruding roof was painted with moons, stars, and planets.

Sound effects added to the drama as battle and storm noises were made by percussion instruments. Lightning and heavenly bodies flew across on wires. Crude powder and paint make-up arrived.

Troupes of owner-actors, journeymen and hirelings acted simple plots and familiar stories, safe choices in the political and religious turmoil. Meanwhile, there was fear of plague being carried by itinerant actors, of civil unrest and women of ill-repute plying their trade. So civil authorities often banned players and refused their entry into a town without an official licence.

Shakespeare earned income as playwright, actor and investor/share-holder in acting companies. In 1576, James Burbage built London's first public theater, known simply as The Theatre. London's Globe (completed 1599) became a showcase for Shakespeare's works and Burbage's company. Indoor private theatres opened – roofed and with less seating capacity than outdoor theatres.

Plays set in 1500-99 include:

Bottom's Dream – Alan Poole

The Clink – Stephen Jeffreys

Henry VIII – William Shakespeare

Luther – John Osborne

A Man for All Seasons – Robert Bolt

Mary Stuart – Friedrich Schiller

Rosencrantz and Guildenstern are Dead – Tom Stoppard

Royal Hunt of the Sun – Peter Shaffer

Vivat! Vivat! Regina! – Robert Bolt

. . . plus numerous Shakespeare plays

Lifestyle: furnishings

Heavy and sparse furniture grew more elaborate, and sideboards became a fashionable way to display plate. Stools or chests were used rather than chairs. On the floor were loose rushes (often full of filth and fleas) or rushes plaited together into a rug. Male servants slept on palettes, taken up during the day. The family sat at the high table, and everyone else at trestle tables – moved to make room for games, dancing, and sleeping. The rich sometimes had Turkish carpets. Feather beds replaced straw mattress. Elaborate four-poster beds were so highly valued as to be left in wills. Baths were considered unhealthy.

Tudor buildings 1500-75

Churches were still largely Gothic but their windows and doors became smaller, and the flattened Tudor arch arrived. The power of the church diminished with the Reformation – and soon the dissolution of the monasteries released large areas of land. Many more secular structures were raised, including farms and labourers' cottages.

The multi-sided oriel window became fashionable, cantilevering out from an upper floor and supported on a bracket or corbel below. With the widespread use of coal, flues, chimneys and enclosed fireplaces were needed to eliminate smoke and now became more common. Chimney stacks were often in groups, and were curved, twisted, and decorated with chequerboard patterns of coloured bricks. Spreading from East Anglia, where it had been introduced from the Low Countries in late medieval times, brick became a popular luxury – often brought back in ships that exported English wool to the Continent, or made by Dutch immigrants in East Anglian brickyards. Hampton Court Palace, and many fine country houses were built in brick.

In the Midlands and northern counties, wooden houses, generally in oak, were more numerous than brick. Timber skeletons were filled in with plaster – or brick, usually in a herringbone pattern. Sometimes the lower storey was built in stone, with wood on the upper storeys. The typical 'black-and-white' Tudor house had whitewashed plaster set between black oak timbers. In towns (where ground-floor space was precious and street frontage might be taxed) the upper storeys often projected above the ground floor.

1500-1599

Grander houses featured impressive gatehouses, displaying a family coat of arms. A broad, low arch was flanked by tall, octagonal towers with false battlements. Indoors, oak panelling might extend from floor to ceiling – and often featured the linen-fold motif – a raised carving that resembled folds of cloth.

Elizabethan buildings 1550-1625

Henry VIII's indulgence and debts meant that by the end of his reign, the country was almost bankrupt. Also, the wool trade was no longer so prosperous, so fewer new buildings arrived. However, under Elizabeth I, there was a return to farming, plus a new optimism and confidence. Wealth re-emerged and British economy revived.

Many small houses and country mansions were built; earlier manors were remodelled and modernised. Now Italian Renaissance and the Dutch influence had an impact as seen in the curved gables. The purely ornamental gatehouse became rare and the open E- shape house arrived, with the vertical line of the E being the main hall, the shorter central line the entry porch and the horizontal end lines kitchens and living areas.

Running the entire length of the upper floor of the main hall, a long gallery served for entertaining, for family gatherings, and exercise; it was also a portrait gallery. It had windows on three sides and fireplaces on the fourth and became the focal point of family life. Its entrance was often embellished with classical columns, heraldic emblems, carvings and ornate decoration.

As brick popularity decreased, chimneys were once again built in stone. Often they resembled classical columns and were square now, rather than corkscrew, but still in groups of two or three. Large windows were now fashionable, made of numerous small rectangular panes separated by slim mullions, with a simple dripstone or classical hood moulding.

Smaller Elizabethan houses evolved slowly as fireplaces and chimneys became more common, and staircases more prominent. Half-timbering was popular, with the timbers now spaced more widely apart so there was space for elaborate infill decoration. A central hall was now floored in, halfway to the roof, creating an upper storey, with a living area and a kitchen on either side.

Both indoors and outside, strapwork was carved in low relief, or moulded in plaster, to make symmetrical geometric patterns. There were also moulded plaster panels, coloured marble (often a black-and-white chequer floor), curvilinear columns, and plaster ceilings that aped Gothic fan vaulting.

In town and country

In the busy narrow streets, banners, signs and washing hung from the overhanging upper storeys. There were stalls selling food, barrels of country beer, dancing bears, pedlars and pickpockets.

Formal knot gardens had small plots of herbs edged with box or bricks. In farming areas, there were windmills, watermills with great circular millstones, hay ricks, vast barns, straw beehives, grazing sheep and some fields still worked in strips.

Historical background
English rulers in this period:

1491-1547 King Henry VIII

1547-1553 Edward VI
1553-58 Queen Mary I
1558-1603 Elizabeth I

1501
Vespucci explores S. American coast.

1517
Cortes conquers Mexico.

1524
German peasants rebel.

1527
Charles V sacks Rome.

1533
Pizarro executes Inca chief Atahualpa.

1534
England breaks with Roman Church .

1542
1st European visitors to Japan.

1543
Copernicus claims earth circles sun.

1544-46
England and France 2-year war.

1547-84
Ivan the Terrible Czar of Russia.

1562
Beginning of slave trade.

1577-80
Drake circumnavigates globe.

1587
Mary Queen of Scots executed.

1588
Spanish Armada defeated.

1597-1601
Irish rebellion.

Timber-frame buildings dominated throughout Western Europe. Black or brown beams were infilled with wattle and daub panels, limewashed white or cream. Upper floors usually projected beyond the ground floors; this characteristic overhang was especially common in towns where ground space was limited and there was tax on occupied floor area.

This farmhouse is also timber-framed, but both the timberwork and in-fill panels are limewashed. The roof and walls are supported on four sets of oak crucks – huge, curved, A-shaped timbers. These divide the farmhouse into five sections, two to house animals and three for domestic use. An open hearth is set in the centre of the domestic hall.

Stone buildings 1500-1599

In stone-rich districts, the local material was used instead of timber or brick. This wealthy farmer's house of 1544 consists of slate-stone and large boulders with a slate roof. The large chimneys were considered status symbols as most rural houses of this era had the fire in the middle of the main room.

Llancaiach Fawr Manor, Rhynmey Valley, South Wales. This is an example of a provincial stone manor house dating from the early 1500s, later improved in the 1600s. Built to be defended, the 1.2m (4ft) thick walls, sturdy doors and small ground floor windows bear testimony to the turbulence of 16th-century Britain.

Elizabethan great houses possessed a symmetrical façade and layout, the plan gradually assuming an E-shape. Other features included a long gallery, an imposing staircase and formal gardens. The 'hall' now became less used for living and became a large entrance area, and other rooms such as the long gallery assumed greater importance.

Hardwick Hall, Derbyshire (1590-97) is an Elizabethan mansion famous for its large mullioned and transomed windows. This feature led to the saying, 'Hardwick Hall, more glass than wall.'

Tudor gateway to St. James' Palace

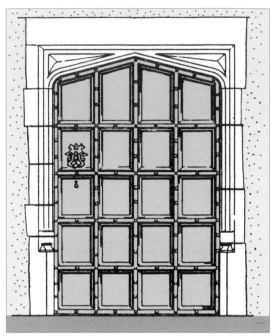

Doorway, Chantmarle, Dorset

Left: *Elizabethan farmhouse hearth*

Below left: *Grand chimney piece, St. James's Palace, London*

Below: *Example of plaster ceiling, Hampton Court Palace*

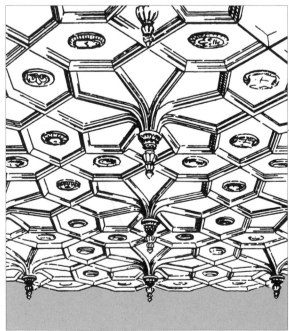

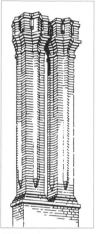

Tudor chimneys

Four-poster bed with drapes

The Tower of London (1086-97) housed many a famous and royal prisoner in the 1500s, including Anne Boleyn and Elizabeth I

In galleons like this, explorers set out to discover new territories. Battles were also fought at sea and the Armada witnessed a huge deployment of Spanish vessels. The Renaissance saw a slowing of naval warfare in Europe and disbanded crews sometimes found a new role as pirates

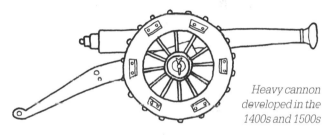

Heavy cannon developed in the 1400s and 1500s

Tudor rose, a useful emblem of the combined white and red roses of the warring houses, united at the end of the War of the Roses

EXAMPLES OF ELIZABETHAN ORNAMENT

Designs taken from wood carving from *(left to right):* Montacute, Somerset; an old chair; wood diaper in the Old Palace, Enfield

European Renaissance 1500-1599

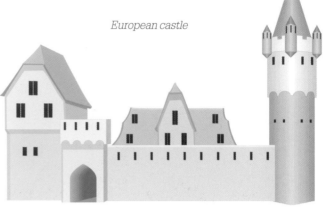

Upper stories of houses overhang the narrow canal with a pinnacled, crenellated building behind.

European castle

European town houses

Ornate designs and details add flourish in the more elegant interiors

Fireplace with mythical figures and two divers supporting mantelpiece

Swiss fountain capital

Statues set in niches at Heidelberg Castle

German doorway (Munich)

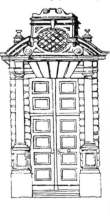

Breton chateau, rebuilt in 1500s with mullioned windows and ornate parapet

German Townhall (Rathaus) 1535-96, essentially Gothic with low arcades and ornate clock set before a steep roof

1600-1699

Puritanism verses opulence

From Puritan restraint to Cavalier extravagance, this was a period of many contrasts. It saw the spread of plague through Europe that confounded medical understanding – side by side with many scientific advances and new inventions. Jacobean styles gradually supplanted the medieval lines.

Theatre development

Theatre reflected the extremes of the century from Cromwell's Puritan restraint to Louis XIV's French court. Permanent theatres now appeared, some with roofs, but the Globe in London burned down when cannon debris set light to its thatch. Under James I, theatres required royal approval and licences. Meanwhile, street theatres still used wheeled carts; pageants by travelling actors or local craftsmen depicted religious spectacles, and actors, musicians, storytellers and conjurers performed at taverns and fairs.

Puritanism halted English drama; in 1642, theatres closed. However, English actors and royalists in exile from Cromwell were influenced by French and Italian theatre as productions there became ever more spectacular, depicting storms, waterfalls and avalanches. In the 1650s, the future King Louis the XIV of France appeared in lavish ballets and masques. Molière founded the Comédie Française and Racine spearheaded tragic plays.

Even after the Restoration in 1660, London city fathers still disapproved of theatre, especially when women appeared on stage for the first time, taking female roles instead of boys. They sought more flattering make-up and used a whitening paste made from fat and white lead with white chalk for powder. Burnt cork served as eyeliner and to darken eyebrows; carmine was used on lips and cheeks. French comedy actors whitened their faces with flour.

Stages grew larger and grander. Inigo Jones designed Whitehall's new royal palace as an elegant backdrop for ornate masques and, for the first time, wings were used. The Italians had a synchronized wing system as machines moved scenery and performers. Magical effects included rolling ocean waves. Theatres were elaborately decorated and lit by chandeliers, oil lamps and candles. Performances still took place in daylight, but lighting created dramatic effects. Below stage level, oil wick footlights floated on water to reduce the fire risk – hence the term 'floats'. In 1674, lights were dimmed for the first time in *The Tempest*.

Now lavish sets created the illusion of space and distance. Inigo Jones bewitched audiences with perspective illusions framed within an ornamental arch – the proscenium arch had arrived and became the standard, dominating Europe's theatre design and separating audience from cast. The area behind the proscenium was used for scenery changes, but the forestage remained the principal acting area. Wings, borders, and shutters arrived in England while machinery above and below stage moved scenery.

Plays set in 1600s include . . .

The Alchemist and *Bartholomew Fair* – Ben Jonson

The Country Wife – William Wycherley

The Crucible – Arthur Miller

Cyrano de Bergerac – Edmund Rostrand, trs. by Christopher Fry

The Devils – John Whiting

The Duchess of Malfi – John Webster

The Libertine – Stephen Jeffreys

Lorna Doone – adapted from R D Blackmore by Jill Hyem

The Misanthrope – Moliere

Roses of Eyam – Don Taylor

The Three Musketeers – adapted from Dumas by Willis Hall

Tis Pity she's a Whore – John Ford

Shakespeare's plays were now considered out of date!

Homes

After the Great Fire, the centre of London was rebuilt to a regular pattern, with wider streets and less overhanging upper stories. There were two, three and four-storey buildings as well as new churches, markets and coaching inns.

Pavement and street lighting gradually arrived, as did new quays and steps down to the river. St Paul's Cathedral rose as the city spread but there were still open fields within a few minutes' walk.

In the grander homes, in town and on country estates, curtains and carpets, as we know them, were rare but wall hangings, tapestries, heavy tablecloths and bed drapes were used extravagently. Interior walls were generally panelled in oak or decorated with moulded plaster panels. Imported marble became fashionable – used for chequered black and white floors and ornate fireplaces.

Broad classical columns, Gothic heraldry, strap ornament and cupids abounded but as the Jacobean period progressed, decorative work became more restrained and sober.

Inigo Jones's fine, new classical façades dominated architecture during this period.

1600-1699

Crime

This was a time of social unrest, poverty, war, religious upheaval – and loose morals – with many extra-marital affairs and prostitutes. (Venice even produced a guide to its top 250 courtesans.) Crime and bribes were common, duelling was socially acceptable and highwaymen robbed wealthy travellers. Paris had a police force of 800 struggling to control 400,000 people. Most towns organised a city watch but generally justice relied on a hue-and-cry system. Major crimes carried a death sentence; minor ones were punished by whipping, the pillory, branding, or the cutting off of body parts.

Science

Serious study required wealth as well as talent and most students had a substantial private income. Astronomers studied astrological charts and chemists were often alchemists, trying to convert lead or base metal into gold. Medical knowledge had progressed little and it was still believed that too much fluid in the body caused diseases, and that plagues were due to planet alignments and foul air. However, many new tools and instruments were arriving, such as the microscope, telescope, pendulum clock, vacuum pump and barometer. Astronomers mapped the visible moon and discovered Jupiter's satellites. Scientists invented calculus and logarithms and experimented with steam.

Work and entertainment

The aristocracy hunted deer, boar, game birds, and foxes. They gambled at cards and horse races, and enjoyed singing, playing the guitar, piano, harpsichord or recorder. The middle classes enjoyed music, science and politics. At clubs, tobacco, coffee and hot chocolate from the New World were discovered. Newspapers were launched in London in 1622 and soon most towns had their own paper broadsheets.

Farmers, craftsmen and labourers worked up to 16 hours a day, 6 days a week. Only on Sundays and religious holidays was there leisure time for theatre, alehouse or blood sports (such as cock fighting, bear or bull baiting and bull fighting), all these forbidden under Cromwell's Protecorate.

Marriage and children

Families were large but there was a high infant mortality rate. Parents arranged marriages and dowries; divorce or separation was rare. The rich might maintain illegitimate children in their households but poorer ones were raised by the Parish unless the father could be charged with the child's custody. The mother might be fined or flogged and run out of the Parish.

Historical background

British monarchs in this period:
James I 1603-25
Charles I 1625-49
Cromwell/Protectorate 1649-60
Charles II 1660-1685
James II 1685-1688
William (and Mary) 1689-1702

1600
East India Company chartered.

1605
Gunpowder plot.

1610
Galileo uses telescope.

1611
Authorized version of Bible.

1613
Russian Romanov dynasty founded.

1618-48
Thirty Years War in Europe.

1620
Landing of *Mayflower* pilgrims.

1632-49
Taj Mahal built.

1638
Galileo explains gravity.

1642-46
English Civil War.

1643-1715
Reign of French Sun-King, Louis XIV.

1644
End of Ming dynasty.

1649
Charles I of England beheaded.

1656
Pendulum clock invented.

1665
Newton announces Law of Gravity.

1665
Great Plague of London.

1666
Great Fire of London.

1692
Witch trials in Salem.

1698
Czar Peter the Great visits England.

Women worked long hours, often in a poor light, at weaving and spinning – to make items for the home or as a source of income

Right: Farmhouses usually had a dairy and butter and cheese were an important supplement to the family needs and revenue

Typical dining tables in a farmhouse and servants' hall

Domestic interiors 1600-1699

Hearth and home became synonymous with imposing, large fireplaces. While these were simple inglenook-style in kitchens and farmhouses, they became very ornate in the richer homes

Domestic life in New England, as elsewhere, centred around the hearth with cooking, spinning and house chores in the living areas and, on farms, chores in the dairy, barns and stable

Partitions and screens became increasingly common in the 16th and 17th centuries. They were usually of oak, and either of chamfered 'stud-and-plank' construction, such as the one shown here, or a similar but narrower and more refined, 'muntin-and board' construction.

In more formal living rooms, interior walls were heavily panelled in oak or decorated with moulded plaster panels

Domestic interiors 1600-1699

The canopy over the four-poster bed protected the sleepers from dust and vermine, and kept them warm
Lady's bed chamber in a manor house

In rustic farmhouse bedrooms, sparse dark oak furniture usually included an enclosed box-style bed. Ground-floor rooms generally had a beaten earth floor.

A timber-framed farmhouse of 1678 with thatched roof. The walls were constructed on a stone plinth to prevent the timber beams from rotting

St Peter's Hospital, (destroyed in World War Two) was a pretty half-timbered house in Bristol

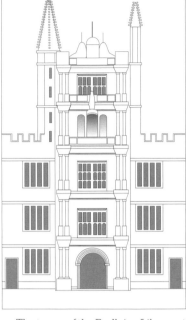

The tower of the Bodleian Library at Oxford is a mix of Gothic and new Renaissance with mullioned windows and elaborate pinnacles

Old Market Hall, Shrewsbury, was raised at the turn of the century and typifies how an arched area set below the main building offered protection from the weather for stall-holders, shoppers and produce

A Jacobean mansion: this, the west façade of Charlton House in Kent, was built 1607-12. Steps lead up to a fine central entrance, with balustrades here and along the roof

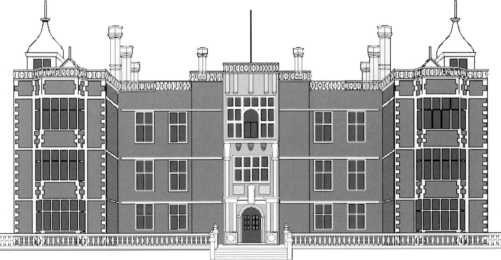

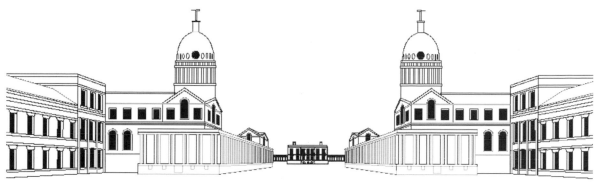

Inigo Jones taught his masons how to interpret his drawings accurately and introduced elegant Italian Renaissance styles to England. The Royal Hospital at Greenwich, begun as a palace by a pupil of Inigo Jones, was completed by Sir Christopher Wren 1616-35

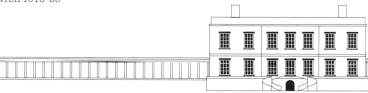

Inigo Jones built the Queen's House in Greenwich, 1616-35, for James I and his family

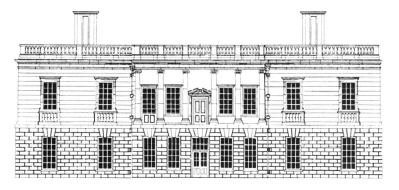

Its rectangular shape, strict classical lines and Palladian symmetry were very innovative at the time and influenced domestic design thereinafter.

Built 1616-35, the Covered Bridge at Wilton exhibits decorative Rennaisance-style details. Features like this added architectural elegance to landscaped gardens

York Watergate in London was a river entrance to the Duke of Buckingham's home in 1626 when the river was a major highway

London 1600-1699

Above: *Shoreditch, London, in 1642*
Below: *Bow Bridge, London*

Below: *View of London at the time of the Great Fire, 1666*

Above: *The Great Plague Pit in Aldgate, London*

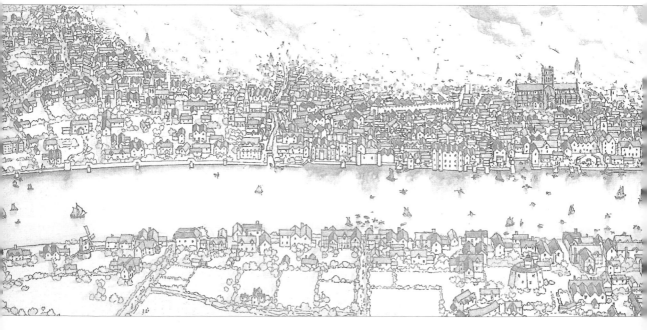

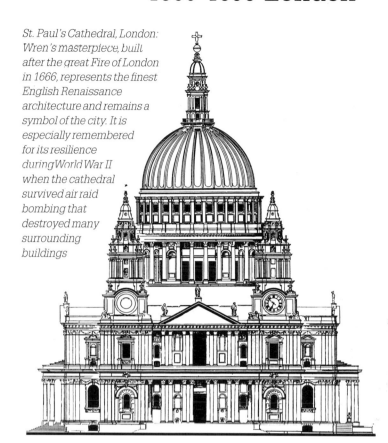

St. Paul's Cathedral, London: Wren's masterpiece, built after the great Fire of London in 1666, represents the finest English Renaissance architecture and remains a symbol of the city. It is especially remembered for its resilience during World War II when the cathedral survived air raid bombing that destroyed many surrounding buildings

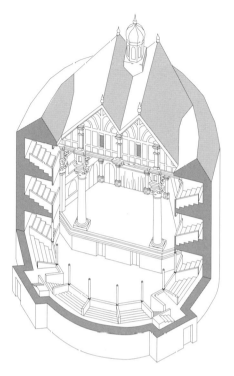

The first Globe Theatre in London burned down when debris from a cannon used in a play set light to its thatch. This second theatre was built in 1614

Palaces 1600-1699

This was a time of flamboyant palaces that, throughout Europe, made a clear statement of the owners' wealth and extravagence. Versailles [right] with its vast network of state rooms, its Hall of Mirrors and fine landscaped gardens exudes opulence – as do many other palaces and stately homes that followed in its wake. Although most rich aristocrats were displaced during the French Revolution in the next century, many of France's fine buildings survived and later housed leaders of the new order. Napoleon I, for example, resided at Fontainebleau, as did a succession of war leaders during World War II

Versailles Gardens present a formal landscape but also have 'secret' enclosed areas

1700-1799

The age of Revolutions

Classical, Baroque and Rococo styles brought elegance into fine homes and cities, side by side with growing poverty in the meaner streets while, in the country, the Agrarian Revolution marked a more scientific approach to farming. The later decades witnessed the great turmoil of the American War of Independence and French Revolution.

Theatre development

After the Glorious Revolution of 1688, there was a resurgence of Puritanism and sentimental comedy, with satires that mocked upper class manners and tragedies featuring great heroes. In 1737, the English government imposed strict censorship laws that halted dramatic development for 150 years. Professional companies were led by actors such as David Garrick (1717-79) who chose the plays.

Theatres were more comfortable now and had permanent roofs. In 1700, there were 3 theatres in Paris; by 1750, there were 20. Tiers of pit, boxes, and galleries appeared; seats in boxes, offering some privacy, were popular for the élite. A 3-hour theatre evening included orchestral music, a prologue, a full-length play and an afterpiece (pantomime, farce, or comic opera). Variety turns (magic acts, singing, dancing, acrobatics, and animal tricks) took place between acts. Meanwhile, early operas emerged with sung dialogue, in Italy. Baroque costumes were rich and exotic, especially in masques, with fabulous creatures, gods, mermaids and monsters.

Silk screens, and coloured glass chimneys on oil lamps, lit the stage in rich scarlet and blue. Transparent backcloths and gauze allowed a glimpse of magical figures behind. Panoramas and dioramas appeared. Meanwhile, moving perspective sets had detailed scenic backdrops and wings that changed to create different scenes. This grew even more detailed and pronounced, with rows of cut-outs, one behind the other, lit by candlelight.

In the 1760s wings and shutters were mounted on carriages on rails below the level of the stage. Another system developed with grooves above and below the wings – the stage opened in several places to allow scenery to slide in and out. Actors were transported into position on bridges, manipulated by intricate stage machinery. Backcloths and borders on rollers were flown above the stage; meanwhile, pyrotechnics, and dramatic fog and fire effects, grew ever more popular.

Plays set in 1700s

Amadeus – Peter Shaffer

The Beaux Stratagem – George Farquhar

The Beggar's Opera – John Gay

Les Liaisons Dangereuses – Christopher Hampton

Lock up your Daughters – adapted by Bernard Miles and Lionel Bart from Fielding's *Rape upon Rape*

The London Merchant – George Lillo

Madness of George III – Alan Bennett

The Recruiting Officer – G Farquhar

The Rivals – R B Sheridan

The Scarlet Pimpernel – adapted from Baroness Orczy by Beverley Cross

The School for Scandal – R B Sheridan

She Stoops to Conquer – O Goldsmith

A Tale of Two Cities – Several plays and musicals, adapted from Dickens

Tom Jones – adapted from Henry Fielding by Joan Macalpine

The Way of the World – William Congreve

Lifestyle

In Europe, where 85% of the population were rural peasants or serfs, the rich grew richer and the poor faced greater hardship. In England many peasant farmers were driven from their land through its enclosure and new machinery. French aristocrats claimed hunting rights, dues, fees, and tithes. Many landlords controlled law and justice – and revolts were easily crushed. But new industries and social revolution would destroy the old order at the end of the century.

The French Revolution

The American War of Independence focussed attention on new ideals and then the French Revolution, eight years later, had a huge impact throughout the Western world. Designed to make execution more humane, the guillotine soon became a symbol of tyranny. 40,000 people travelled on the Paris tumbrils to die.

Guillotine facts and figures:
Total weight – 580 kilos (1278lb)
Blade weight – over 40 kilos (88.2lb)
Side post height – just over 4m (14ft)
Blade drop – 2.3m (88 inches): at 7m (21ft) a second
Power at impact – 400 kilos (888lb) per sq. inch
Decapitation took 1/50th of a second but it could take up to 30 seconds for consciousness to be lost

Homes and furnishings

In fashionable towns and spas, such as Bath, buildings were classical-temple style. Terraces, streets and squares were fronted with Palladian villas and façades.

Inside, columns, pilasters and doorways were framed with columns and pediments and all observed Classical proportions. Baroque boldness in line and ornament was followed by lighter Rococo in about 1740, when this introduced graceful details – on mirror frames, chimney pieces, furniture, wallpaper, textiles and ceilings. There were good knotted carpets or imported Oriental rugs. Fitted carpets might be made of broad strips and a border sewn together – or floors might be painted with a design or patterned with black and white squares.

Curtains were now more elaborate, and festoons became popular. Fabrics were lightweight, with delicate Rococo designs. Walls were decorated with rich fabrics stretched across the wall, or down to the dado; flock paper imitated Italian silk velvet. Wooden panelling was painted white, stone or olive green.

In the country house, a central entrance hall usually had an impressive staircase and might sport coats of arms and suits of armour. Upstairs rooms were used not only for sleeping but also for sewing, writing, and reading.

After dinner, while the men enjoyed brandy and cigars, the ladies retired to the withdrawing room. This drawing room, also used for dances or card games, would have musical instruments, carved mahogany chairs, a sofa with curved back and scroll arms, chairs with walnut legs and brass-studded covers, a tilt-top tripod table with piecrust rim, a petit point firescreen and a needlework rug. Servants were kept at a distance, housed in their own wing and summoned by long-distance cords connected to bells.

Mahogany was the main wood; richly carved pieces included marble-topped tables on gilded pedestals with birds, animals or female figures. Paintings in gilded frames held family portraits. Libraries had leather-upholstered chairs, globes on stands, and billiard tables.

Meanwhile, the homes of the poorer classes remained largely unchanged although the details were now less medieval and houses were being built with more permanent materials.

Fine estates

European monarchs and the aristocracy built fine palaces and mansions and enjoyed a grand lifestyle. In England, many landed gentry remained on their country estates where their large houses dominated the surrounding countryside. They also had houses in London, in which they stayed when fulfilling Parliamentary duties, but their true homes were in the country.

Health and medicine

If harvests were bad, hunger and famine struck the poor while all were susceptible to diseases like influenza, smallpox, typhoid and yellow fever. Beds were often full of bed bugs, and rats and fleas still spread infection. However, hygiene was better understood after Frank's statistics on public health were published (1767) and in 1796, Jenner introduced a vaccine against smallpox.

Anatomy was now studied and students sometimes resorted to paying body-snatchers to keep up the supply of cadavers. Surgery and obstetrics received more serious scientific attention, as did dentistry – false teeth were being made in Germany in 1756.

Historic background

William III	1694-1702
Anne	1702-1714
George I	1714-1727
George II	1727-1760
George III	1760-1820

1700s
Agricultural Revolution in England.

1701-13
War of Spanish Succession.

1706
Act of Union: England and Scotland.

1739-41
War between England and Spain.

1741
Handel composes *The Messiah*.

1756-63
Seven Years War.

1765
Watt builds steam engine.

1768-79
Captain Cook's voyages to Pacific.

1775-1781
American War of Indepence.

1789
Mutiny on *The Bounty*.

1789-1795
French Revolution. Louis XVI guillotined in 1793.

1796-1815
Napoleonic wars.

1798
Britain and Russia fight France.

Farmhouses and cottages 1700-1799

Weatherboarding was widely used on cottages and barns in south-east England as it was a cheaper alternative to tile-hung and brick-faced walls. Softwoods were painted, but elm and oak were usually left bare

Timber-frame construction continued to be used on smaller buildings in areas where timber was more readily available than stone – such as on this house in Wiltshire, England

This Cornish cottage, like many humble rural buildings, was built of cob – a mixture of mud and straw built up in layers. Cob buildings were limewashed, tarred at the base, and usually had thatched roofs.

This limewashed-stone cottage is typical of those found in most parts of Wales throughout the 1700s, and similar to those of Scotland and Ireland. A large gabled fireplace was a common internal feature; later cottages often had another, smaller fireplace on the opposite gable

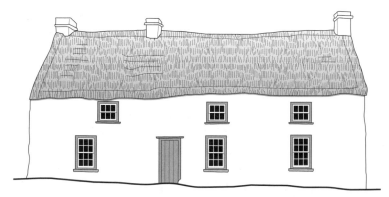

An Irish farmhouse of the early 1700s, with limewashed-stone walls and a thatch roof

Dresser of the early 1700s with pewter plates, and the late 1700s with blue and white china

Stone dwelling with limewashed walls

Above: *Farmhouse kitchen with dairy equipment that includes a large, oak cheese press*
Right: *Living area of a cottage with small window*

Cottage sleeping quarters were often behind makeshift partitions and in half-lofts accessed by a ladder. Bed covers were generally hand-worked quilted blankets

Grand houses 1700-1799

A Palladian-style facade

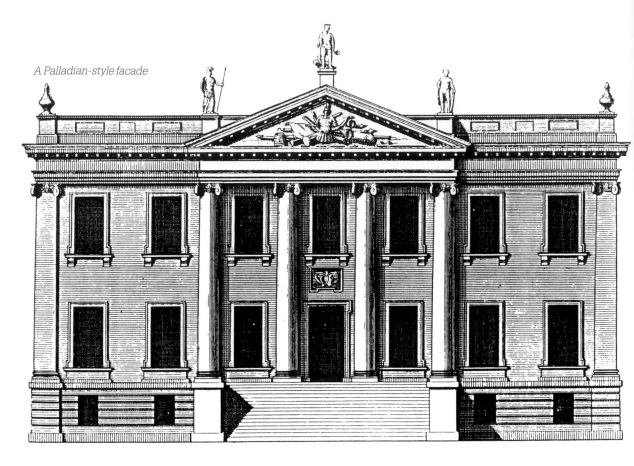

Superb wrought-iron gates, steps and balustrades, grand drives, bridges and lakes added distinction to French palaces and chateau

Portraits of the family, as well as scenes of battle and mythology, were subject matter for a plethora of painting. Ceilings were especially ornate, while plaster and wood surfaces and surrounds were also worked in intricate detail

Ornate and grandiose features included domed ceilings and fine sweeping staircases with balustrades and columns – a setting fit for Cinderella's entrance to the ball

An avid search for knowledge and understanding now had a more scientific basis. Many libraries and studies sported terrestial and celestial globes. When Sir Isaac Newton died in 1727, he was given a state funeral

Beds 1700-1799

Refined four-poster beds were elaborate with richly carved wood and voluminous drapings, that in Regency times were sometimes arranged like a tent

Box beds continued to be popular in cottages and farmhouses. Some, like this one, were completely enclosed. They kept the warmth in and the cold out, and afforded some privacy in cramped and crowded homes

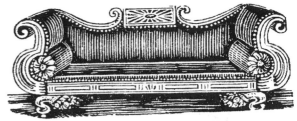

Graceful curving lines and scrolled ends on couches and sofas show a Grecian influence

An ornate timepiece might be hung on the wall or be built into a free-standing piece of furniture

Grand staircases were generally straight flight with landings. The balusters were uniform and slight, with two or even three to a tread

Intricate carving and a high level of decoration create a rich effect

Better roads and improved suspension made coach and carriage travel far more comfortable in the 1700s. Elegant private carriages were the owners' status symbols and the royal coaches are still used for state occasions in England

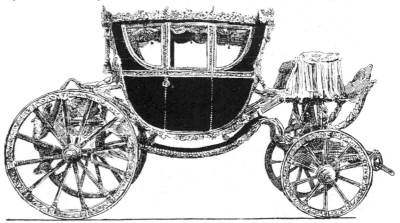

Fireplaces and mirrors 1700-1799

In grand homes, fireplaces were of elegant design and, like the furniture, were both robust and decorative. Mantelpieces displayed extremely elaborate, ornate surrounds

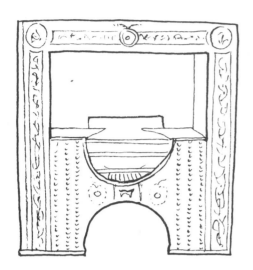

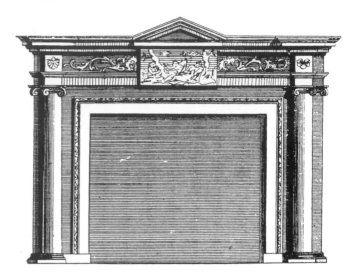

The huge inglenook fireplace was the focal point in farmhouses and cottages and was where all the cooking was done

Mirrors had profuse ornament, with plants and birds incorporated into swirling candle holders and Rococo decoration

Doors, windows and gates 1700-1799

The sliding sash window, in various shapes and sizes, was used on almost every type of building throughout the 1700s

Simple ledged-and-boarded doors, with latches and strap hinges, were used everywhere in farms, cottages, and the attics and service areas of grander houses

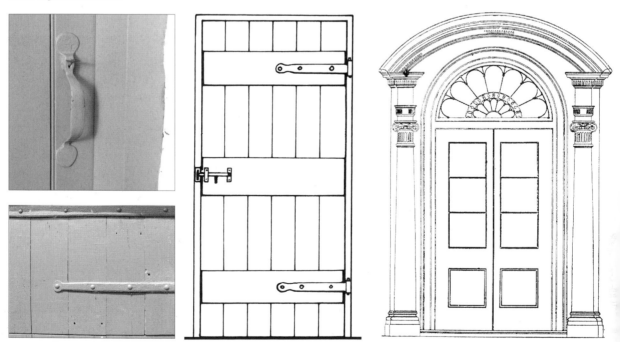

Ornamental gates to homes, gardens and parks became a feature and have remained so until today

In grand homes, steps with wrought-iron balustrades led up to generous doorways with elaborate canopies – often in deep shell shapes – with pediments supported on columns, and tanlights

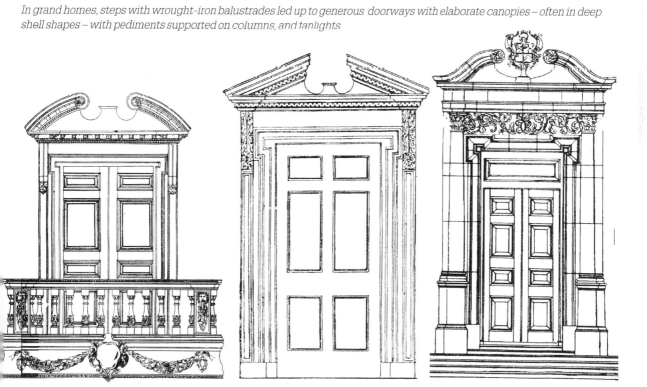

England 1700-1799

Sweeping crescents and circuses formed fine, dignified vistas in spas and cities such as Bath, Brighton and Cheltenham

10 Downing Street has an unpretentious, Georgian-style frontage. The original late 17th - century house was refronted in the 1700s. The Street itself was developed by George Downing after his return from America's War of Independence

Mansion House, London, is a Palladian creation by George Dance I and was built to serve as both mayoral office and home

Chinese (and to a lesser degree, Japanese) art styles had an enormous influence on ceramics, furniture, fabrics and decoration of all kinds in the 1700s

United States of America 1700-1799

State Capitol, Richmomd, Virginia 1789-98

Georgian styling crossed the Atlantic and was popular until the American War of Independence (1775-1781) after which obvious English styles were rejected in some parts of the USA

Westover in County Virginia, built from 1730-33, is a fine example of a distinguished plantation house

The Capitol, Williamsberg, Virginia, has been rebuilt in its original brick Georgian style of 1701

1777 Union Flag

1776 Congress flag

1795 Union flag

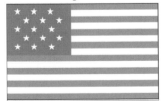

1800-1899

Imperialism and industry

In this time of great empires, of Napoleon and Queen Victoria, there is increased industrial surge and new scientific discoveries, plus exciting advances in transport – with canals, rail and motor cars. Dire conditions prevail in factory and mines and America fights its Civil War. As the century closes, women enter the professions and the Boer War is fought.

1800-1899

Theatre development

In the 1800s, the Romantic movement in drama was led by Goethe and Schiller while Italian dramatists introduced operatic libretti. Melodrama, farce, and comedy were enjoyed – and the Magic Lantern arrived. In 1816, gaslight was first used in a theatre in the USA: now at last all the stage could be seen with equal clarity and main characters no longer had to dominate the downstage area. Slide projection appeared in the 1820s to create patterns and colours on the stage. Vast spectacular effects – such as sinking ships – amazed audiences In 1822, the Paris Opera created real waterfalls and fountains on stage.

Meanwhile, fading and cross-fading helped gauze transformations to create fire effects, setting suns and starlit skies. In 1816, limelight arrived, first as a follow spot but soon used for sun and moon beams; by the end of the century, a large theatre might implement thirty limelights. As the first proper spotlights appeared, performers needed better stage make-up, now produced commercially for the first time. From the 1850s, there was also greater naturalism in acting, scenery and costumes. Mirror flats soon arrived, as did the hydraulic lift (in 1854) and by the 1860s, a prototype cyclorama.

As the railway system expanded, so did touring companies, especially in the US. Circuses now had animal acts and clowns, as well as acrobats, and become travelling theatre in the 19th century, spreading in line with the growth of the railways. Extravagant Grand Opera, Gilbert and Sullivan light operettas, and drama now offered audiences enormous choice. Melodramas were highly popular but vanished once cinema delivered its life-like, sensational material. In 1879, a US theatre was the first to install electric lighting. In 1883, in Gilbert and Sullivan's *Iolanthe*, the fairies wore illuminated stars in their hair – hence the term 'fairy lights'. Meanwhile, Wagner reformed theatre architecture – introducing sloping, fan-shaped seating, giving an equal view of the stage to all. The 1880s Symbolist movement was followed by realism as the century closed.

Plays set in 1800-1839

Frankenstein – adapted from Mary Shelley by Tim Kelly

Great Expectations – adapted from Charles Dickens by Hugh Leonard

Mansfield Park – adapted from Jane Austen by Willis Hall

Murder of Maria Marten – Melodrama by Brian J Burton

Peer Gynt – Henrik Ibsen

Plays set in 1840-1869

Barnum – musical by Coleman, Stewart and Bramble

Camille – Pam Gems

A Christmas Carol – plays and musicals adapted from Dickens

The Heiress – adapted from Henry James by R and A Goetz

Jane Eyre – adapted from Charlotte Brontë by Willis Hall

Lady Audley's Secret – melodrama by Brian J Burton

A Month in the Country – Turgenev

Sweeney Todd the Barber – various adaptations from G D Pitt

Treasure Island – adapted from R L Stevenson by Miles, Coe and Wilson

Trelawny of the 'Wells' – Pinero

Woman in White – adapted from W Collins by C Cox

Plays set in 1870-1899

Can Can – musical by Cole Porter and Abe Burrows

Charley's Aunt – Brandon Thomas

The Cherry Orchard – Chekhov

Count Dracula – adapted from Bram Stoker by Ted Tiller

Gaslight – Patrick Hamilton

The Government Inspector – N Gogol

Hedda Gaber – adapted from Henrik Ibsen by John Osborne

The Hound of the Baskervilles – adapted from Conan Doyle by T Kelly

The Importance of Being Earnest – Oscar Wilde

Lark Rise – adapted from Flora Thompson by Keith Dewhurst

The Magistrate – A W Pinero

The Matchgirls – musical by Bill Owen and Tony Russell

The Seagull – Anton Chekhov

The Turn of the Screw – adapted from Henry James by Ken Whitmore

The Wind of Heaven – Emlyn Williams

Lifestyle

Working people generally rented accommodation in town houses, terraced rows, farms and cottages – or lived in as servants. Homes were still lit by candles and water collected from pumps – often carrying diseases such as cholera. Meanwhile, many slaved in factories, mills, mines, and potteries up to sixteen hours a day. Some suffered dreadful injuries in machines, developed lung illnesses or were paralysed from working long hours, breathing in dust and noxious fumes. Chimney-sweep boys often had cancers caused by soot. The unjust 1838 Poor Law incarcerated old and young in the parish workhouse, providing only gruel and bread to eat and often separating families. By contrast, the wealthy moved from town, to spa, to seaside resort and to country house.

Solid, robust furniture included round tables on pedestals with scrolls or carved paws, chaise longues, ottomans, round-backed sofas and balloon-back chairs with curved woodwork. Maple veneers and inlays, Classical maidens, elaborate borders, swags of flowers and foliage, Egyptian motifs, fringes, tassels and braids abounded. Furniture often stood in the middle of a room below cascading cut-glass chandeliers, large mirrors, sporting pictures and scenes by Turner. Glass domes covered birds on branches. Walls were hung with needlepoint and embroidery, featuring mottoes or floral designs.

Servants' rooms were fitted with cheap furniture – cane bedroom chairs, painted pine chests of drawers, and cast-iron beds. Well-to-do families now sometimes had a bathroom but most washed and bathed in the bedroom, using basins and hip-baths filled with jugs of water carried up by a servant.

As the century drew to a close, homes were lit with gas – or occasionally, electricity by the 1890s. Electric street lighting arrived in 1878 in London. Coal-fired stoves and new kitchen equipment made cooking easier. Piped water reached town houses in the 1870s, and soon purpose-built bathrooms arrived – with washbasin and roll top, cast-iron bath. However, poorer homes and rural houses still had an outside earth closet; in cities, toilets might be shared by over a hundred people.

Now canals and railways threaded the nation, and family visits to the seaside became fashionable. By the turn of the century, mangles and primitive washing machines had arrived and most families had a Kodak camera. Meanwhile, the Arts and Crafts movement and Art Nouveau spearheaded new design.

Historic background

1805
Battle of Trafalgar.

1807
England abolishes slave trade.

1808-15
Napoleonic Wars:
Battle of Waterloo 1815.

1812-14
War of American independence.

1829
Stephenson's *Rocket*.

1840
Morse Code devised.

1848
Revolution in Paris.
Karl Marx's *Communist Manifesto*.

1849
Gold Rush in California.

1851
Crystal Palace, Great Exhibition.

1854-56
Crimean War.

1855
Livingstone discovers Victoria Falls.

1859
Darwin's *Origin of the Species*.
First internal combustion engine.

1861-65
American Civil War.

1863
President Lincoln abolishes slavery in US but he is assassinated in 1865.

1870
Papal power ends; Italy unified.

1876
Bell demonstrates telephone.
Battle of Little Big Horn in US.

1877
Phonograph invented by Edison.

1879
Zulu War.

1887
Motor car engine and gramophone.

1888
Jack the Ripper terrorises London.

1890
Eiffel Tower built.

1899-1902
Boer War in Africa.

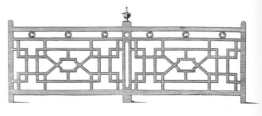

Left: *Example of a fine Regency town house*
Top right: *Chinese-style railings were fashionable*
Above left: *Regency entrance doorway*
Above right: *John Nash's Royal Pavilion at Brighton, England, was commissioned by the Prince Regent and is mainly 'Hindoo' style on the outside and Chinese on the inside*

A Regency ball interior setting in a stage production

Public buildings of the period, such as The British Museum (1823-47, above) and The National Gallery (1834-38, below) are characterised by symmetrical façades and entrances with pedimented porticos

An industrial worker's terraced house at the beginning of the century

Britain **1840-1869** 1800-1899

Buckingham Palace

In 1761 George III purchased the palace for his wife. It was remodeled in 1826 and in 1837, and Queen Victoria moved here and made it the prime Royal residence. In the courtyard, a triumphal Marble Arch was erected to commemorate the British victories at Trafalgar and Waterloo. But this was removed in the 1840s and now stands on the northeast corner of Hyde Park. Queen Victoria's ballroom was once the biggest room in London. The present forecourt of Buckingham Palace was created in 1911

Westminster New Palace (1840-60), generally called the Houses of Parliament, was an influential – and fine – example of the mid-1800s Gothic Revival. A vast complex of buildings, it stands alongside the Thames, and is often regarded as a symbol of London.

The Red House, Bexley Heath, Kent, is inspired by the vernacular and influenced the Arts and Crafts houses of the next generation. It was built from 1859-60 by Philip Webb for his friend William Morris, the famous sociologist and decorative designer.

Above: *Industrial workers' cottages*
Below: *Backyard of a humble urban house with outside privy*

Cast-iron milestone

Corn Mill of 1853

The Crapes Inn on the Thames river, London, was where characters from Dickens' Our Mutual Friend *went to drink 'at the bar to soften the human breast'*

Rear of terraced row of houses

A London East End pub

Suburban, terraced housing for the middle classes were set out on spacious streets. The perspective effect is augmented by the diminishing heights of the many chimneys. (Photographed in the 1960s)

This late-Victorian London theatre has both conventional seating and tables with benches at ground-floor level. The seating at the two higher levels is almost a full circle. Everywhere, the decoration is highly ornate, but especially so on the ceiling

Historical and vernacular styles inspired late-Victorian designs, such as on this small suburban house in the 'Queen Anne' style and (far right) a 'Tudorbethan' country lodge

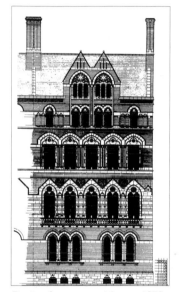

Design for town residence, 1875

Large country house, 1875

Infirmary of 1870

Cottage furnished in late-Victorian style
Stores of 1880s: both window dressing and interiors were cluttered but everything had its place

School of 1880

Above and right: The Supreme Court Building, Washington

Monticello, near Charlottesville, Virginia, was remodelled in a free and imaginative Palladian style from 1796-1808.

Stars and bars Confederate flag 1861

Confederate battle flag 1861

The White House (1829), the official residence of the US Presidents, is in English Palladian style

The United States Capitol (1867), the seat of government in Washington DC, has a superb crowning dome and is a world-wide symbol of the US

An example of a ramshackle, timber tenement building of the mid-1800s. Many immigrants settled in cramp and squalid areas

Skating on public skating lakes, such as this one in Central Park, became extremely popular from the late 1850s

The Tribune Building (1875), New York, was one of the very tall buildings built in the city in the late 1800s

The Statue of Liberty (1886). This is a projected design of 1875: the final pedestal is different and she faces the city, not out to sea

1900-2000

From bicycle to space travel

In a century of escalating change, two world wars spearheaded scientific advance followed by the Cold War which accelerated the space race. Women seized greater control over their lives and careers. As the new millennium dawned, computer technology changed communications fundamentally, even more so as the Internet arrived.

1900-2000

Drama and theatre

Music Hall and Vaudeville in the early decades were followed by the Roaring Twenties, the Charleston, Prohibition, Depression and then two world wars. Theatre, cinema and home wireless offered an escape from a fraught world but the impact of home entertainment reduced live theatre audiences. In the 40s, US musicals included *Oklahoma* and *South Pacific* but many British plays were still the 'drawing-room' variety. Big bands were popular and variety shows featured new stars from forces entertainment. Symbolism, Absurdism, Realism and the Expressionist movement were explored. Absurdism peaked in the 1950s – John Osborne's *Look Back in Anger* (1956) became a focus for 'angry young men'.

Massive technical changes followed in the wake of electric lighting and spotlights. Modern lighting equipment and sound systems became more versatile and manageable while rock-and-roll music spearheaded the growth of electronic sound and sophisticated mixing consoles. Scenery became suggestive rather than realistic.

In the 60s, ensemble theatre evolved plays through explorative work by the actors. Albee and Pinter wrote dark plays. US theatre reflected the rise of minority groups and feminists, anxiety over the Vietnam war and the threat of nuclear holocaust. As the 70s closed, there was a return to naturalism – to ordinary events and characters. Meanwhile clever light and projection and optical illusion reflected abstract art. Pyrotechnics and computers advanced – storing, and coordinating sound and light and using laser beams, holograms, fibre optics, and projection. Batteries of lamps supplied a great intensity of light – but amateur theatre generally still relied on mechanical means.

Many 18th-century theatres were restored; new theatres had high raked seating, thrust stages, or theatre in the round. Some had revolving seating that could mutate from conventional to theatre in the round. Performances flourished in parks and historic sites in summer, while street theatre and festivals reinstated travelling theatre.

Plays set in 1900-1919

A Flea in her Ear – G Feydeau

An Inspector Calls & *When We Are Married* – J B Priestley

Gigi and *My Fair Lady* adapted from Colette /Shaw by Lerner & Loewe

Journey's End – R C Sheriff

The Plough and the Stars – O'Casey

Ross & *The Winslow Boy* – T Rattigan

Plays set in the 20s include:

The Boyfriend – S Wilson

Daisy pulls it off – D Deegan

Juno and the Paycock – S O'Casey

Rookery Nook – B Travers

Plays set in the 30s include:

Anastasia – M Maurette

Cabaret – Kander & Ebb

Cause Célèbre – T Rattigan

Crown Matrimonial – R Ryton

Night Must Fall – E Williams

Prime of Miss Jean Brodie – J P Allen

Private Lives/This Happy Breed – Noel Coward

Plays set in 1940s include:

Arsenic and Old Lace – J Kesselring

Blue Remembered Hills – D Potter

Death of a Salesman – Arthur Miller

The Diary of Anne Frank – Goodrich & Hackett

The Long and the Short and the Tall – Willis Hall

The Night of the Iguana – T Williams

Plays set in 1950s include:

Billy Liar – Waterhouse & Hall

Shadowlands – W Nicholson

A Taste of Honey – S Delaney

Under Milk Wood – Dylan Thomas

West Side Story – Bernstein & Robbins

Plays set in 1960s

Alfie – B Naughton

Hair – Ragni, Rado and MacDermot

The Homecoming – Pinter

The Knack – A Jellicoe

Who's Afraid of Virginia Woolf? – Albee

Plays set in 1970s include:

Absurd Person Singular – Ayckbourn

A Chorus Line – Kirkwood, Dante, Hamlisch & Kleban

Cracks – M Sherman

Miss Saigon – Boublil, Schonberg & Mally Jnr.

Plays set in 1980s–1990s include:

A Chorus of Disapproval / Way Upstream – A Ayckbourn

The Full Monty – S Beaufoy

Three Tall Women – E Albee

Lifestyle – in the early decades

Art Nouveau styles were followed by Arts and Crafts. Wicker, cane and bamboo arrived and furniture was painted in soft colours or gilt highlights. Armchairs and sofas had chintz or damask covers. There were tapestry fire screens, Tiffany lamps and female bronzes. The Orient inspired screens and rugs. Stained glass was popular – and gramophones with conical shells. Travel was by motor car, bus or rail – often to the seaside. Male and female servants were kept apart: women slept in the attic and men in the basement. Maids carried up jugs of hot water for a weekly dip in a tin bath.

As Modernism introduced more severe functional styles, Art Deco explored racy and geometric shapes but by the 30s, Modernist Art Deco emerged – with affordable items manufactured en masse. Soon furniture was bulbous, highly polished or with shiny upholstery. Home decoration included sunray and stepped motifs and wild spashes of colour. The Bauhaus influence brought tubular chrome-plated chairs and tables. Vacuum cleaners and the wireless gained momentum. There was a building boom in the 1920s and 30s and the German Volkswagen was the most popular car in the world.

1940s and 50s lifestyle

By 1941, women worked in munitions, aircraft factories, the Land Army – and soon the forces. Food and clothes were rationed. Bombs fell, and cities burned. After the war, 200,000 people in Britain had to be rehoused while some stayed on in temporary 'prefabs' that became permanent homes Utility furniture from 1943 was basic but well designed. In suburbia, many semi-detached homes had the latest cocktail cabinet, real or mock leather sofas, standard lamps and black bakelite telephones. After the war, home improvement and DIY arrived.

By the 50s, reproductions of paintings such as Constable's *Haywain* and Shepherd's elephants became popular, set above the coal fire (with electric or gas fires elsewhere). Chairs and coffee tables had a steel rod base and ball feet. Abstract spidery black lines or squiggles decorated fabrics, upholstery and Formica surfaces. There were pouffes and scattered rugs, portable record players, transistor radios and slender curving tulip chairs and tables. Few homes had telephones but there were many public phone boxes. Television was a new luxury and some families saw the Coronation on TV but these were not common until the late 50s. This was the time of rock and roll, skiffle, beatniks, scooters and jukeboxes in coffee bars. A few homes had fridges but there were no home freezers and few cars. Many trains were still steam driven and most people rode bicycles to work or school.

1960s and 70s

Now most homes had twin-tub washing machines, spin dryers and refrigerators. Supermarkets and launderettes spread and the Mini became the most popular small car as new motorways halved journey times. Tower blocks rose as old buildings were demolished to make way for modern shopping centres and multi-storey car parks. New semi-detached houses were bigger – often with a garage and large gardens. Through dining room-lounges arrived – and open-plan kitchens, shelving dividers, central heating, and Pop Art's brash colours and shapes. In 1964 Habitat introduced good, affordable design into the home. Psychedelic and ethnic designs and king-size beds arrived. By the end of the 60s, TVs were universal. Colour TVs arrived in 1967 but these were expensive and colour did not reach all three channels until 1969.

In 1972, the British Museum's Tutankhamun exhibition led to great interest in Ancient Egypt. Now long-pile shag carpets were fitted in rooms with Laura Ashley's nostalgic country styles with flower sprigs and tiny patterns on fabric, wallpaper and furnishings. Fitted kitchens were common and automatic washing machines arrived in the 70s. TVs were set in cabinets and colour TVs became affordable, but still not commonplace. The first low-priced TV games and videocassette recorders appeared and there were supermarkets even in small towns. Jumbo jets doubled passenger capacity and foreign holidays became even cheaper, especially to Spain.

80s and 90s

Old industries died; new technologies and Western economy boomed but the gap between rich and poor grew with unemployment. There were compact discs, camcorders and fitted kitchens – with built-in ovens and microwaves. Mix-and-match sofas, chairs and corner seating replaced three-piece suites. Polished wooden floors, wicker storage boxes, scatter

1900-2000

rugs, futons and garden barbecues became popular. Vast out-of-town superstores arrived. Computers reached homes, offices, and schools – and finally, the Internet appeared. Discount air fares reduced the cost of Atlantic flights. AIDS became a huge threat but people lived longer and there was a strong focus on health, diet and exercise.

Historic background

1903
Wright Brothers aeroplane.

1908-27
Ford's Model T car.

1909/12
North Pole/ South Pole reached.

1914-18
First World War.

1917/1918
October Revolution in Russia/Tsar and family murdered.

1920-1933
Prohibition in USA.

1922
Irish Free State set up.
Tomb of Tutankhamun discovered.

1927
Television invented.
Lindbergh crosses Atlantic.

1930
Gandhi leads revolt in India

1932
Atom split.

1936
In UK, Edward VIII abdicates.

1936-39
Spanish Civil War.

1939-45
World War Two.(Dunkirk evacuation and Battle of Britain in **1940**).

1941
Japanese attack Pearl Harbor.

1945
War ends. Atomic bombs used.

1946
1st electronic computer.

1947-49
India independent; New state of Israel; Ireland republic declared; Communist victory in China.

1949
Germany splits into East & West.

1950-53
Korean War.

1951
1st commercial digital computer.
1st color television broadcast.

1953
Elizabeth II crowned (inherited throne 1952).
Hilary & Tensing climb Everest.

1954
McCarthy's Communist witch-hunt.

1956
Suez War.

1957
Sputnik launched by Russians.

1961
Gagarin is 1st man in space.

1962
Cuban missile crisis.

1963
President Kennedy assassinated.

1967
First heart transplant.

1968
Martin Luther King, Jr. assassinated.
Robert Kennedy assassinated.

1969
US lands 1st men on moon.

1973
US withdraws from Vietnam.

1975-79
Spcecraft visit Venus, Mars & Jupiter.

1976
Apple II personal computer.

1978
First 'invitro' (test-tube) birth.

1982
War in Falkland Islands.

1986
Nuclear disaster at Chernobyl.
Space shuttle *Challenger* explodes.

1989
Berlin Wall (raised 1961) comes down.

1990-91
Gulf War.

1991
USSR's formal end.

1992
Civil war in former Yugoslavia.

1997
US Pathfinder lands on Mars.

1998
Northern Ireland peace.

1999
War in Kosovo.

1900 bakehouse, Aberystwyth – closed 1924

Tailor's shop 1896 enlarged 1920s

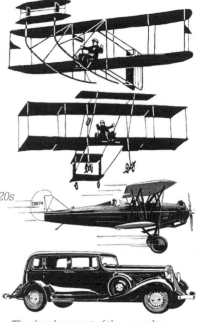

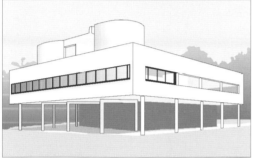

Le Corbusier's Villa Savoye, built 1929-30

In general, his period was one of great change and contrasts: aeroplanes, motor cars and skyscapers arrived. Designs by architect Le Corbusier today appear 30 or 40 years ahead of their time, but in poorer areas and rural communities, fashion had little impact.

The development of the aeroplane was rapid from flimsy flying machine to military aircraft. The car soon mutated into many new designs

A miner's home in 1925 has Christmas decorations and family portraits Below: a miner's banner c. 1916 and the Worker's Institute building where the library provided an opportunity to improve knowledge and education: the style reflected wealthy homes.

Golden Gate Bridge, San Franciso, 1930

Firth and Forth Bridge, 1930s

Above: *A typical 1930s semi-detached house*

Below: *Tiffany-style lamps typify the late 20s and early 30s this type of design also appeared in fabrics, stained-glass doors and window panels*

Above: *the American timber-framed home c.1930s*
Below: *The simplistic buildings were constructed without any embellishments c.1936*

British 'pre-fab', emergency housing, 1948: some are still in use today. The basic 'utility' furniture in the living room, kitchen, bathroom and bedroom was manufactured en masse in the late 40s and early 50s to serve the needs after the War

Cars of the 50s outside Paramount Studios, USA

American car of the 50s with sweeping lines

The ever-popular French 2CV of the 60s

The ultimate British-manufactured Rolls Royce of the 1960s

Volkswagen Beetle was highly popular from the 1930s through four decades

Right: *Typical 1955 middle-class living room with antimacassars on chair backs, small television set, china cabinet and mantel clocks*

The Twin Towers New York 1970

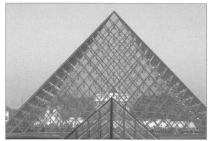

Three pyramids at the Louvre 1989

As leisure time became more available, leisure centres were built and sports such as skiing, wind-surfing, waterskiing, and snow boarding increased in popularity, as did keeping fit

Shopping centres and hotels had large open internal areas. Dining and bedrooms were luxurious

Japan dominated the motorbike revival

Left: *Steamlined built-in kitchen/diners replaced the utilitarian type of kitchen* [above] *with water heater and surface electricity. Video recorders and colour TV became standard. A loft conversion* [right] *with roof windows added an extra room – often a bedroom but in this case, a study.*

Offices moved out of cities into new, smart buildings with large receptions

Huge sports stadiums were built round the world. The package holiday and reduced air fares made flying abroad available to everyone

Left : out of town supermarkets were vast

New cathedrals (as here in Brazil and America) offered a chance for architecural innovation

From mobile home to 'executive' detached, decor was either ultra-modern or nostalgic.

Living today 1900-2000

Skyscrapers arrived in every city although a few, like Paris, managed to maintain a lower profile. Car ownership and traffic jams increased and space exploration became 'the norm'

Exteriors

- Woodland and forest
- Field, moor and meadow
- Stream, river and lakeland
- Seaside, shore and sand
- Gardens
- Mountain scenery
- Clouds and sky

This second section of the book looks at specific settings, rather than historical periods. Much will depend upon individual play directions and, in certain cases, may involve just a single scene or act, rather than an entire play. As with the historical part of the book, the items selected can be only a representation of potential sets – in this first section, a selection of exterior scenes.

Woodland and forest Exteriors

Individual trees offer an inspirational variety of shapes, with patterns of light and shade, and forests can create many different atmospheres, from wild and menacing to peaceful idyll. The classic European woodland is of mixed varieties with pools of light between; heavier forestation may be dense conifers. Obviously, the seasons bring their changes and Autumn colours can create especially dramatic settings.

Set in woodland and forest . . .

Alice through the Looking Glass – adapted from Lewis Carroll by C. Dane and R. Addinsell

Dear Brutus – J.M Barrie

The Gypsy's Revenge – Michael Lambe

Midsummer Night's Dream – Shakespeare

The Lion, the Witch and the Wardrobe – various adaptations from C S Lewis

Robin Hood – several versions

Many fairy tales and pantomimes include forest scenes such as *Babes in the Wood, Goldilocks, Hansel and Gretel, Red Riding Hood* and *Sleeping Beauty.*

Oak leaf

Sycamore leaf

Elm leaf

Fir cones

Mushrooms

Fern

Field, moor and meadow Exteriors

These pastoral scenes are the epitome of British countryside and the backdrop for many plays. Some productions set in farms may also require general field backdrops. There arc also plays set in wilder moorland.

Set in field, hill and meadow . . .

Peter Rabbit and other adaptations from Beatrix Potter

Blue Remembered Hills – Dennis Potter (wood, field, and barn)

Cider with Rosie – Laurie Lee

Far from the Madding Crowd – adapted from Thomas Hardy by Matthew White

Hound of the Baskervilles – adapted from Sir Arthur Conan Doyle by Tim Kelly

Lark Rise – adapted from Flora Thompson by Keith Dewhurst

Lorna Doone – adapted from R D Blackmore by Jill Hyem

The Murder of Maria Marten or *The Red Barn* – Brian J Burton

Sisterly Feelings – Alan Ayckbourn

Tess of the D'Urbervilles – adapted by Michael Fry from Thomas Hardy

Winnie the Pooh – A A Milne

Wuthering Heights – adapted from Emily Brontë by Charles Vance

Thistle

Foxglove

Butterfly

Poppy

Stream, river and lakeland Exteriors

Water can be a very evocative element. Still waters are undoubtedly easier to depict close up but sound and light can help to create or augment moving water effects.

Set by river, stream and lake . . .

Lorna Doone – adapted from R D Blackmore by Jill Hyem

Neville's Island – Tim Firth

Showboat – Oscar Hammerstein II

Swan Lake – ballet by Tchaikovsky

Venus Oberved – Chrstopher Fry

The Water Babies – adapted from Charles Kingsley by Willis Hall

Way Upstream – Alan Ayckbourn

Ugly Duckling – A A Milne

Wind in the Willows – adapted from Kenneth Grahame by John Morley

Seaside and shore Exteriors

Sea settings can be tranquil or wild, a windswept British resort or a tropical desert island. Many a play is set by a beach or with a view of the sea beyond a garden or through the window.

Children's theatre and pantomime also include numerous versions of *Peter Pan, Robinson Crusoe Treasure Island* and *The Water Babies* that feature sea and seaside settings.

Set by sea or shore . . .

The Island – James Saunders

The Admirable Crichton – J M Barrie (desert island)

The Sea – Edward Bond

Shirley Valentine – Willy Russell

The Tempest – William Shakespeare

Under Milk Wood – Dylan Thomas

When I was a Girl I used to Scream and Shout – Sharman MacDonald (rocky beach and promenade)

The Winter Guest – Sharman Macdonald (promenade and beach)

Women on the edge of HRT – Marie Jones (Irish beach)

Gardens Exteriors

Gardens often provide play settings –
from the present-day surburban
backdrop through rambling cottage
gardens and formal landscapes to
fantastic escapist gardens.

Set in the garden . . .

Alice Through the Looking Glass –
adapted from Lewis Carroll

Brideshead Revisited – adapted from
Evelyn Waugh by Roger Parsley

The Cherry Orchard – Chekhov

Cold Comfort Farm adapted by
Paul Droust from Sheila Gibbons

Fall – James Saunders

The Gazebo – Alec Coppel

The Importance of Being Earnest –
Oscar Wilde

Round and Round the Garden –
Alan Ayckbourn

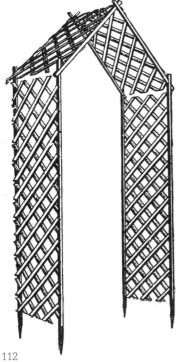

Gardens Exteriors

Mountains make inspiring backdrops and may form a complete set or be viewed through a window. The scenery may include flowery meadows on alpine slopes or be desolate jagged peaks.

Set in mountain scenery ...

Heidi – several versions, adapted from Johanna Spyri

Maid of the Mountains – Frederick Lonsdale, George Posford and Bernard Grun

The Sound of Music – adapted from Van Trapp by Rogers and Hammerstein

Valley of Echoes – Brian Way

White Horse Inn – Ralph Benatzky

Mountain scenery Exteriors

Many scenes need to incorporate the sky which may be just part of the scenery or an entire effect in its own right – perhaps used on a cyclorama and lit in different ways or with projected lighting or cloud or star effects. Skies are one of the most evocative elements in the scenographer's portfolio.

Clouds and sky Exteriors

International guidelines

- The Far East
- Africa
- India
- Australia
- Northern/Central Europe
- Paris
- London
- New York
- Venice
- Southern Europe
- South America

This section explores a variety of International settings - cities, nations and continents. The images range from landscapes to cottage to city street and provide a flavour of many places around the world, depicting the old and the new, the familiar and the exotic.

The Far East International guidelines

A good number of plays have been set in the Orient but often the geographical and national barriers become blurred in escapist musicals or children's stories. Serious plays, war dramas and the like certainly need realism. Good oriental images also appear on page 76.

Set in the Orient or East

Aladdin – Numerous versions

Chu Chin Chow – Musical by Oscar Asche and Frederick Norton

Flower Drum Song – – Musical by Rodgers and Hammerstein

The Imperial Nightingale – Nicholas Stuart Gray

The King and I – Musical by Rodgers and Hammerstein

Madame Butterfly – Opera by Puccini

Made in Bangkok – A Minghella

Mikado – Gilbert and Sullivan

Miss Saigon – Musical by Boublil, Schonberg and Mally

Turandot – Bertolt Brecht (China)

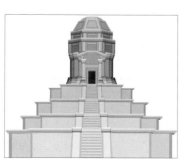
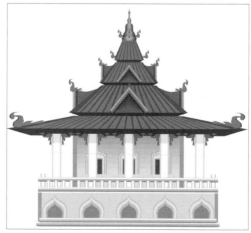

Africa International guidelines

Here are just a few possibilities from a vast continent that ranges from desert to savanna, rivers, lakes, mountains and bazaars.

Set in Africa or the Middle East . . .

Desert Song – Sigmund Romberg, Frank Mandel and Oscar Hammerstein II

Map of the Heart – William Nicholson

The Mummy's Tomb – Ken Hill

Murder on the Nile – Agatha Christie (set on a Nile steamer)

Night and Day – Tom Stoppard

Peer Gynt – Henrik Ibsen (scenes in Sahara, Morocco and Cairo)

Ross – Terence Rattigan

Egypt, Cario

Egypt

India International guidelines

Whether set in the jungle or an Indian Raj veranda, these evocative settings all exude heat and the magic of exotic far-flung places through both landscape and buildings. Several military plays are set in India or the jungle, too.

Set in India or the jungle . . .

Indian Ink – Tom Stoppard

Jungle Book – various adaptations from Kipling

The Long, the Short and the Tall – Willis Hall

Man is Man (Man equals Man) – Bertolt Brecht

Privates on Parade – Peter Nichols (Malaya)

International guidelines **Australia**

This is yet another continent of great contrasts and often features on round-the-world trips to represent the opposite side of the globe: the Sydney Opera House is a particularly distinctive, recognisable building while Ayers Rock is a dramatic natural rust-red feature, standing in isolation in the vast outback.

Set in Australia ...

A Hard God – Peter Kenna

Jack and the Baked Bean Stalk – Judith Prior

Mind if I Sit Here – Paula Williams

Our Country's Good – adapted from Thomas Keneally by Timberlake Wertenbaker

Northern/Central Europe International guidelines

Northern Europe has a wide variation of landscape, cities and cultures. The selection here can be only a starting point to inspire set ideas as each country merits an entire chapter – were there space!

Set in Northern/Central Europe ...

Anna Karenina – Tolstoy (Russia)

Diary of Anne Frank – adapted by Frances Goodrich and Albert Hackett (Holland)

Germinal – adapted from Emile Zola by William Gaminara (Northern France)

The Little Mermaid – several versions and a ballet adapted from Hans Christian Andersen (Denmark)

On the Razzle – Tom Stoppard (Vienna)

The Mother – Bertolt Brecht (Russia)

Peer Gynt – Henrik Ibsen (Scandinavia)

Norwegian fjords

The Little Mermaid, Denmark   *Dutch windmills*

Dutch tulips   *Traditional Dutch cottage and meadow*

Moscow

Czechoslovakia   *Czechoslovakia*

Scottish castle   *Scottish castle*   *Scottish village cottages*

International guidelines **Northern/Central Europe**

British medieval castle

Mud and thatch cottage, western Britain

Thatched farmhouse, early 1700s, western Britain

Early industrial cottage, Great Britain

Victorian industrial cottage, Great Britain

Stonehenge, Great Britain

British red telephone box

Alpine village

Neuschwanstein, Bavaria

Mid-European street

Bavarian village, Germany

Alpine valley

Paris International guidelines

While the plays selected here are largely set in the past, modern Paris frequently features in revues, comedy sketches and as an icon for Europe and the Continent.

Set in Paris ...

Gigi – Colette

The Hunchback of Notre Dame – adapted from V Hugo by G Sullivan and J T Wallace

The Prodigious Snob (or *Le Bourgeois Gentilhomme*) – Moliere

The Miser – Moliere

Nana – adapted from E Zola by O Wymark

Picasso at the Lapin Agile – Steve Martin

The Scarlet Pimpernel – adapted from Baroness Orczy by B Cross

A Tale of Two Cities – adapted from Dickens by Matthew Francis

The Three Musketeers – adapted from Dumas by Willis Hall

Arc de Triomphe

Arc de Triomphe

La Grande Arche de La Défense

La Grande Arche de La Défense

Palace at Versailles, near Paris

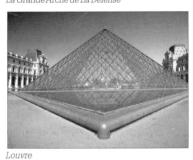
Louvre

Sacró Coeur

Notre Dame

Pompidou Centre

London International guidelines

From Dickensian workhouses to the Millennium Eye, London makes a fascinating backdrop. The Tower and Westminster suggest its history and many plays focus on royalty though the centuries.

Set in London . . .

Crown Matrimonial – Royce Ryton

Dick Whittington – several versions

The Drunkard or Down with Demon Drink! – melodrama by Brian J Burton

Follow that Girl – musical by Renolds and Slade

High Profiles – Woodrow Wyatt

Iolanthe – Gilbert and Sullivan

Jack the Ripper – Ron Pember and Denis de Marne

A Man for All Seasons – Robert Bolt

Oliver – musical by Lionel Bart

The Strangeness of others – Nick Ward

Also, Shakespeare histories such as *Henry VIII* and Dickens adaptations.

Dickensian riverside scene

Aldgate, 1830

Buckingham Palace

Changing the guard

Houses of Parliament, Big Ben and Westminster Bridge

10 Downing Street (Prime Minister's residence)

Tower Bridge

Royal Albert Hall

Public house

MI6 headquarters

Millennium Bridge

Westminster Abbey

Tower of London

Trafalgar Square and National Gallery

St Paul's Cathedral

London Eye

Lloyds of London building

New York International guidelines

This exciting metropolis has strong icons – the Statue of Liberty, Chrysler Building or Empire State Building, Times Square night lights and streets jammed with yellow taxis. Central Park features too, with its quieter ambience, and many hotels and city apartments are depicted in plays when the view from the window may indicate the New York atmosphere. Dingier apartments, iron balconies and fire escapes create less glitzy settings in *West Side Story*.

Plays with scenes set here:

42nd Street – Stewart, Bramble, Warren and Dubin

A Chorus Line – Hamlisch, Kleban, Dante, Bennett and Kirkwood

Barefoot in the Park – Neil Simon

Guys and Dolls – Frank Loesser and Abe Burrows

I'm not Rappaport – Herb Gardner (Central Park)

June Moon – Kaufman and Lardner.

Night Watch – Lucille Fletcher

Plaza Suite – Neil Simon

New Amsterdam 1630s

Manhattan Island

Times Square

Squalid tenements, early 1800s

Sataue of Liberty

Chrysler Building

Flatiron Building

Woolworth Building

Typical brownstone terraces

Empire State Building

Metropolitan Museum of Art

Typical fire escapes

Guggenheim Museum

Central Park

Venice International guidelines

This most romantic of cities has played a fine backdrop to many real-life dramas through history as well as the fictional ones. A port and city, built on piles, it was a trading republic from the 10th century. Superb buildings, gondolas and the light play on water can be both beautiful – and menacing, as in Daphne du Maurier's *Don't Look Now*.

Set in Venice ...

Death in Venice – adaptations of the work by Thomas Mann

Geometry in Venice – Michael MacKenzie

The Gondoliers – Gilbert and Sullivan

Losing Venice – John Clifford

The Merchant of Venice – William Shakespeare

Southern Europe International guidelines

Plays range through Ancient Greek and Roman times, the Italian Renaissance, and Victorian Grand Tours to today. Often the atmosphere is redolent of Mediterranean warmth but may also depict warring nations.

Set in Southern Europe . . .

Barber of Seville – Rossini (Italy)

Carmen – opera by Bizet (Spain)

Dona Rosita the Spinster or the Language of Flowers – F G Lorca (Spain)

French without Tears – T Rattigan

The Life of Galileo – B Brecht (Italy)

Passion Killers – John Godber (Spain)

Private Lives – Noel Coward (S France)

Roman Fever – adapted from Edith Wharton by Hugh Leonard (Rome)

Scapino – F Dunlop and J Dale (Naples)

Shirley Valentine – Willy Russell

Sufficient Carbohydrate – Dennis Potter (Greek villa)

Surprise Package – D. Greenwood and D Parkes (Spain)

Coastal village, south of France

Typical hillside town, mid to south France

Buildings, French-Italian border

Narrow street, S France / N Italy

Michelangelo's David, Florence

Ponte Vecchio, Florence

St Peter's Basilica and Piazza San Pietro, Rome

Piza

Italian steps

Sagrada Familia church, Barcelona

Mosque, Istanbul

Southern Europe has many Roman edifices

Spain

Example of Islamic style in Spain

Spanish / Portuguese countryside

Rural courtyard

Mediterranean harbour

Spanish / Portuguese beach scene

Spanish / Portuguese village

Rhodes, Greece

Greek harbour village

Greek village

Lindos, Rhodes, Greece

Greek arch and steps

South America International guidelines

An exotic continent, threaded by the Amazon river and the Andes, where jungle, vast grasslands, icy mountain peaks and the edge of Antarctica provide a wide range of landscape. Mexico, to the north, has been the setting for Westerns . . .

Set in South America . . .

Guys and Dolls –
Frank Loesser and Abe Burrows

Night of the Iguana –
Tennessee Williams

The Royal Hunt of the Sun –
Peter Shaffer

Tilting Ground – Guy Hibbert

Mountain scene, Columbia

Andean mountains, Chile

Balcony window, Columbia

Columbian street

Mountain scene, Venezuela

Chilean church

Mexican church

Mayan pyramid and temple, Mexico

Amazon, Brazil

Rainforest, Brazil

Machu Picchu, Peru

Special areas

- Wild West
- Fairgrounds
- Military scenes
- Trains and stations
- Shopping
- Fairytale and escapist
- Snowy scenes

Many stage designs depict specific settings and need images that do not fall neatly into the book's earlier categories of Historical, Exterior or International settings. The following section provides a selection of ideas and reference illustration for a miscellany of popular settings for plays and entertainment – these include the Wild West, trains and fairy-tale imagery.

Wild West Special areas

A wide variety of plays demand Wild West settings – which might incorporate the rocky landscape, prairie, deserts with cacti, goldmines, saloons, banks, street scenes and the Native American encampment.

Set in the Wild West . . .

Annie Get your Gun – Musical by Irving Berlin and Herbert & Dorothy Fields

Calamity Jane – Musical adapted for stage by Charles K Freeman, Sammy Fain and Paul Francis Webster

Hiawatha – Michael Bogdanov

Destry Rides Again – Musical adapted from Max Brand by Harold Rome and Leonard Gershe

Oklahoma – Rodgers and Hammerstein

Fairgrounds Special areas

Fairgrounds are exciting places, with gaudy colours, flashing lights, music and noise; they can be both magical and menacing and appear in as many thrillers as love stories. Fairs also feature in various pantomimes and children's stories such as *Pinocchio* and *Robin Hood*.

Set in fairgrounds or circus . . .

Barnum – Cy Coleman and Mark Bramble

Bartholomew's Fair – Ben Jonson

Carousel – Rodgers and Hammerstein

War and its edge of danger have given rise to numerous dramas through the ages. Many Shakespeare plays include battles such as Agincourt in *Henry V* and the Wars of the Roses in *Richard III*.

Sets with a war/military bias . . .

Hamp – John Wilson

Journey's End – R C Sherriff

The Long, the Short and the Tall – Willis Hall

Mother Courage and her children – Bertolt Brecht

Not about Heroes – Stephen MacDonald

Not with a Bang – Mike Harding

Observe the Sons of Ulster Marching towards the Somme – Frank McGuinness

Oh, What a Lovely War! – Theatre Workshop Charles Chilton

Privates on Parade – Peter Nichols (Malaya)

Trains and stations Special areas

Melodrama of course, may often involve a fair maiden being tied to a railway track, while numerous Wild West shows include rail and train incidents: some plays have scenes that are set inside railway carriages.

scenes with trains and stations

Anna Karenina – Tolstoy

The Ghost Train – Arnold Ridley

The House of Mirth – adapted from Edith Wharton by Dawn Keeler (Grand Central, New York)

Moscow Stations – Stephen Mulrine

Murder on the Orient Express – Agatha Christie

Once in a Lifetime – Moss Hart and G S Kaufman (scenes in a Pullman car)

The Railway Children – adapted by Dave Simpson from E Nesbit

The Winter Wife – Claire Tomalin

A Word from Our Sponsor – A Ayckbourn

New York, Grand Central Station

London, Liverpool Street Station

Shopping Special areas

These busy sets may require aisles, stalls, or shelves full of books, fruit, antiques or whatever, to establish the venue – or it might be an exterior street scene with shop windows.

Plays with scenes set in shops or markets . . .

84, Charing Cross Road – adapted from Helene Hanff by James Roose-Evans (bookshop)

Half a Sixpence – adapted from H.G. Wells' *Kipps* by Beverly Cross and David Heneker (draper's shop)

American Buffalo – David Mamey (Chicago junk shop)

Hobson's Choice – Harold Brighouse (boot shop)

Orpheus Descending – Tennessee Williams (dry goods store and confectionery

Pygmalion by Bernard Shaw, adapted as *My Fair Lady* by Lerner and Loewe (Covent Garden market)

Sweeney Todd – many versions (barber's shop)

What Are Little Girls Made Of? – Peter Coke (antique shop)

Victorian shops

Burlington Arcade, London

Liberty's, London

Tiffany's, New York

Arcade, London

Macy's, New York

Fairytale and escapist Special areas

Fairy stories offer a wonderful opportunity for imaginative sets. Many a fairy story is set in the Forest or the Orient and so the images in these sections should be checked out, too.

Classic fairy tales include...

Beauty and the Beast (and the Disney musical)

Cinderella

Dick Whittington

Jack and the Beanstalk

Little Red Riding Hood

Pied Piper

Puss in Boots

Sleeping Beauty

Snow White

Grimm Tales – adapted by C A Duffy and T Supple

Peter and the Wolf – adapted from Prokofiev

The Lion, the Witch and the Wardrobe – adapted from C S Lewis by G Robbins

Toad of Toad Hall – Adapted from K Grahame by A A Milne and H Fraser-Simson

Wizard of Oz – adapted from L Frank Baum

Snowy scenes Special areas

Stage snow scenes can be particularly beautiful, often combining special snow effects with scenes of frozen lakes, mountains or trees.

Plays and ballets with snow scenes . . .

The Lion, the Witch and the Wardrobe – various adaptations from C S Lewis

The Nutcracker Suite – ballet by Tchaikovsky

The Snowman – adaptations from Raymond Briggs

The Snow Queen – adapted by Ron Nicol from Hans Christian Andersen

Whale – David Holman

Useful addresses and suppliers

UK

A + M Hire Ltd
The Royals
Victoria Rd
London
NW10 6ND
T 020 8233 1500
F 020 8233 1550
E mark@amhire.com

Albemarle of London
74 Mortimer Street
London
W1N 7DF
E albemarle.productions
@virgin.net
W www.albemarle-
london.com

ASG Stage Products
Redgate Road
South Lancs Industrial
Estate
Lancashire
WN4 8DT
T 01942 718347
F 01942 718219

Blackfriars Scenery
Limited
33 Bear Lane
London
SE1 0UH
T 020 7928 8413
F 020 7261 1994
E staging
@compuserve.com

The Border Studio
Riverside Mill
Level Crossing Road
Selkirk
TD7 5EQ
T 01750 20237
F 01750 20313
E info@borderstudio.com

By 4 Production Ltd
86 Vulcan Mill, 1st Floor,
Bradley Hall Road,
Nelson,
Lancashire
BB9 8HS
T 01282 695959
F 01282 344619

Bower Wood
Production Services
Unit 5, The Billings,
3 Walnut Tree Close
Guildford,
Surrey
GU1 4UL
T 01483 300926
F 01483 450926
W www.bowerwood.com

Get Set Scenery
Unit 3A
John Withey Properties
Off Bedwas Road,
Caerphilly
CF83 3GF
T 029 2088 8990
F 029 2088 5994
E corporatedisplays
@freenet.co.uk
W www.getsetscenery.
co.uk

Ideal Staging & Events
11A Reepham Road,
Norwich
NR6 5LD
F 01603 403035
T 01603 403035
E info@ideal-uk.com
W www.ideal-uk.com

John Dent
Engineering Co. Ltd
1402a Clocktower Road
Isleworth
Middlesex
TW7 6DT
T 020 8560 4414
020 8568 2444
F 020 8847 4582
W info@
johndentengineering.com

Old Times Furnishing
Unit 1
Powergate
Volt Avenue
London
NW10 6PW
T 020 8961 1452
F 020 8961 1462
E inquiries
@oldtimesuk.com

Perry Scenic Limited
Unit D&E
100 Dudley Road East
Oldbury
West Midlands
B69 3EB
T 0121 552 9696
F 0121 552 9697
E info@perryscenic.com
W www.perryscenic.com

PW Stage
Productions Ltd
Cadec House
1 & 2 Cadec Trading Estate
Beaks Road, Bearwood
Birmingham
B67 5RS
T 0121 4343041
F 0121 4343042

Scene Two Hire
18 - 20 Brunel Road
London
W3 7XR
T 020 8740 5544
F 020 8743 2662
E inquiries
@scene2hire.co.uk
W www.scene2hire.co.uk

Set Pieces
Unit 1
Powergate
Volt Avenue
London
NW10 6PW
T 020 8838 1100
F 020 8838 2200
E inquiries
@setpieces.com

Superhire
1-4 Bethune Road
London
NW10 6NJ
T 020 8965 9909
F 020 8966 8107
E props@superhire.co.uk
W www.superhire.co.uk

USA

Pook Diemont
& Ohl, Inc.
701 East 132nd St. Bronx,
NY 10454
T 718-402-2677
F 718-402-2859 fax
E info@pdoinc.com

Rose Brand
75 Ninth Avenue
New York, NY 10011
T 212-242-7554
F 212-242-7565
and
10856 Vanowen Street
N. Hollywood
CA 91605
T 818-505-6290
F 818-505-6293
E info@rosebrand.com
W www.rosebrand.com

Scenic Source
PO Box 831394
Richardson
TX 75083
T 972-994-9227
F 972-994-9818
E info@scenicsource.com

Schell Scenic Studios,
Inc.
841 South Front Street
Columbus
OH 43206
T 614-444-9550
F 614-444-9554
E info@schellscenic.com
W www.schellscenic.com

Secoa
8650 109th Avenue North
Champlin
Minnesota 55316-3789
T 800-328-5519
F 800-898-4756
E catalog@secoa.com
W www.secoa.com

Syracuse Scenery &
Stage Lighting Co., Inc.
101 Monarch Drive
Liverpool
NY 13088
T 315-453-8096
800-453-SSSL
F 315-453-7897

Tru-Roll Inc.
622 Sonora Avenue
Glendale
California 91201
T 818-240-4835
800-989-7516
F 818-240-4855
E www.truroll.com

United Stage
Equipment, Inc
PO Box 667
110 Short St
Hartselle
AL 35640
T 800-227-5407
F 256-773-2586
E use@hiwaay.net

Europe

Arjan's
Show-Biz Centre
P.O. Box 368
2920 AJ Krimpen a/d Yssel
Holland
T 0800 731 8849
(Freephone)
F 0031 180 519171

Other useful contacts

Amateur Dramatics
and Operatics Dot Com.
The online worldwide
directory of Amateur
Dramatic and Operatic
organisations

Amateur Stage
Magazine published
monthly by Platform
Publications
Hampden House
2 Weymouth Street
London
W1N 3FD
UK
T 0207 636 4343
F 0171 636 2323
E cvtheatre@aol.com

NODA
National Operatic &
Dramatic Association
58-60 Lincoln Road
Peterborough
PE1 2RZ
UK
T 0870 770 2480
F 0870 770 2490
E everyone@noda.org.uk

Periods and styles

Year	Style	Principal woods	British monarchs	British periods	French periods
1500	Gothic 1500-1620	Oak period to c.1700 but 1750 in the provinces		Tudor-Gothic	
1510					
1520					
1530					
1540					
1550					
1560			Elizabeth I 1558-1603	Elizabethan	Renaissance
1570					
1580					
1590					
1600					
1610			James I 1603-25	Jacobean	Louis XIII 1610-43
1620	Baroque c.1620-1700				
1630			Charles I 1625-49	Carolean	
1640					Louis XIV 1643-1715
1650			Commonwealth 1649-60	Cromwellian	
1660			Charles II 1660-85	Restoration	
1670					
1680			James II 1685-88		
1690		Walnut period c.1690-1735	William & Mary 1688-94	William & Mary	
1700	Rococo c.1695-1760		William III 1694-1702	William III	
1710			Anne 1702-14	Queen Anne	Régence 1715-23
1720			George I 1714-27	Early Georgian	Louis XV 1723-74
1730			George II 1727-1760		
1740		Early mahogany period c.1735-70			
1750	Neo classical c.1755-1805	Satinwood 1740-1800			
1760			George III 1760-1820	Georgian	
1770		Late mahogany period c.1770-1850			Louis XVI 1774-93
1780					
1790					
1800	Empire c.1799-1815				Directoire 1793-99
1810					Empire 1799-1815
	Regency c.1812-30	Rosewood 1810-50		Regency	
1820			George IV 1820-30		Restauration 1815-30
1830	Eclectic c.1830-80		William IV 1830-37	William IV	Charles X 1820-30
1840		Walnut 1840-60	Victoria 1837-1901	Victorian	Louis Philippe 1830-48
1850					
1860					2nd Empire 1852-70
1870					
1880	Arts & Crafts c.1880-1900	Rosewood 1880-1900			3rd Republic 1871-1940
1890		Satinwood 1880-1920			
1900	Art Nouveau c.1890-1920		Edward VII 1901-10	Edwardian	
1910					
1920					

152

German periods	Italian periods	Low countries	Spain/Portugal	USA periods	
Renaissance to c.1650	Cinquecento 1500-1600 High Renaissance 1500-1630	Renaissance	Renaissance		**1500**
					1510
					1520
					1530
					1540
			Plateresque		1550
	Baroque 1560-1700				1560
		Baroque			1570
					1580
					1590
				Early Colonial	**1600**
					1610
					1620
			Herrara		1630
					1640
Renaissance/ Baroque c.1650-1700					1650
					1660
			Chirriguera		1670
					1680
				William & Mary	1690
Baroque c.1700-30	Rococo			Dutch Colonial Queen Anne	**1700**
			Churrigueresque		1710
					1720
Rococo c.1730-60		Rococo			1730
					1740
Neo-classicism c.1750-1800	Venetian			American Chippendale	1750
					1760
					1770
					1780
	Empire			Early Federal 1790-1810	1790
Empire c.1800-15		Empire		American Directoire 1798-1804	**1800**
Biedermeier c.1815-48		Neo-Gothic	Fernandino 1814-33	American Empire 1804-15	1810
		Rococo revival		Later Federal 1810-30	1820
Revivale c.1830-80			Isabellino 1833-1870		1830
		Historical renaissance		Victorian	1840
					1850
					1860
					1870
Jugendstil c.1880-1920 and Biedermeier 1880-1920	Gusto Floreale				1880
		Art Nouveau		Art Nouveau c.1890-1920	1890
					1900
					1910
	Stile Liberty				1920

British rulers

Rulers of England

Saxons

Egbert	827-839
Ethelwulf	839-858
Ethelbald	858-860
Ethelbert	860-865
Elthelred I	865-871
Alfred the Great	871-899
Edward the Elder	899-924
Athelstan	924-939
Edmund	939-946
Edred	946-955
Edwy	955-959
Edgar	959-978
Edward the Martyr	975-975
Ethelred the Unready	978-1016
Edmund Ironside	1016

Danes

Canute	1016-1035
Harold I Harefoot	1035-1040
Hardicanute	1040-1042

Saxons

Edward the Confessor	1042-1066
Harold I	1066

House of Normandy

William the Conqueror	1066-1087
William II	1087-1100
Henry I	1100-1135
Stephen	1135-1154

House of Plantagenet

Henry II	1154-1189
Richard I	1189-1199
John	1199-1216
Henry III	1216-1272
Edward I	1272-1307
Edward II	1307-1327
Edward III	1327-1377
Richard II	1377-1399

House of Lancaster

Henry IV	1399-1413
Henry V	1413-1422
Henry VI	1422-1461

House of York

Edward IV	1461-1483
Edward V	1483
Richard III	1483-1485

House of Tudor

Henry VII	1485-1509
Henry VIII	1509-1547
Edward VI	1547-1553
Mary I	1553-1558
Elizabeth I	1558-1603

Rulers of Scotland (to 1603)

Malcolm II	1005-1034
Duncan I	1034-1040
Macbeth	1040-1057
Malcolm II Canmore	1058-1094
Donald Bane	1093-1094
Duncan II	1094
Donald Bane (restored)	1094-1097
Edgar	1097-1107
Alexander I	1107-1124
David I	1124-1153
Malcolm IV	1153-1165
William the Lion	1165-1214
Alexander II	1214-1249
Alexander III	1249-1286
Margaret of Norway	1286-1290
Interregnum	1290-1292
John Balliol	1292-1296
Interregnum	1296-1306
Robert I (Bruce)	1306-1329
David II	1329-1371

House of Stuart

Robert II	1372-1390
Robert III	1390-1406
James I	1406-1437
James II	1437-1460
James III	1460-1488
James IV	1488-1513
James V	1513-1542
Mary	1542-1567
James VI	1567-1625

(Became James I of England in 1603)

Rulers of Wales (to 1282)

Wales was usually divided into separate kingdoms or principalities. Five important rulers ruled the whole (or most) of Wales:

Rhodri Mawr	820-878
Hywel Dda	890-950
Gruffudd ap Llywelyn	1007-1063
Llywelyn the Great	1173-1240
Llywelyn the Last	1246-1282

(defeated by English King Edward I, 1282)

Rulers of Britain

House of Stuart

James I	1603-1625
Charles I	1625-1649
Commonwealth	1649-1660

House of Stuart (Restored)

Charles II	1660-1685
James II	1685-1688
William III and Mary II	1689-1694
William III	1694-1702
Anne	1702-1714

House of Hanover

George I	1714-1727
George II	1727-1760
George III	1760-1820
George IV	1820-1830
William IV	1830-1837
Victoria	1837-1901

House of Saxe-Coburg

Edward VII	1901-1910

House of Windsor

George V	1910-1936
Edward VIII	1936
George VI	1936-1952
Elizabeth II	1952-____

Prime Ministers and Presidents

British Prime Ministers

Sir Robert Walpole	1721-1742
Earl of Wilmington	1742-1743
Henry Pelham	1743-1754
Duke of Newcastle	1754-1756
Duke of Devonshire	1756-1757
Duke of Newcastle	1757-1762
Earl of Bute	1762-1763
George Grenville	1763-1765
Marquess of Rockingham	1765-1766
Earl of Chatham	1766-1767
Duke of Grafton	1767-1770
Lord North	1770-1782
Marquess of Rockingham	1782
Earl of Shelburne	1782-1783
Duke of Portland	1783
William Pitt	1783-1801
Henry Addington	1801-1804
William Pitt	1804-1806
Lord Grenville	1806-1807
Duke of Portland	1807-1809
Spencer Perceval	1809-1812
Earl of Liverpool	1812-1827
George Canning	1827
Viscount Goderich	1827-1828
Duke of Wellington	1828-1830
Earl Grey	1830-1834
Viscount Melbourne	1834
Sir Robert Peel	1834-1835
Viscount Melbourne	1835-1841
Sir Robert Peel	1841-1846
Lord John Russell	1846-1852
Earl of Derby	1852
Earl of Aberdeen	1852-1855
Viscount Palmerston	1855-1858
Earl of Derby	1858-1859
Viscount Palmerston	1859-1865
Earl Russell	1865-1866
Earl of Derby	1866-1868
Benjamin Disraeli	1868
William Gladstone	1868-1874
Benjamin Disraeli	1874-1880
William Gladstone	1880-1885
Marquess of Salisbury	1885-1886
William Gladstone	1886
Marquess of Salisbury	1886-1892
William Gladstone	1892-1894
Earl of Roseby	1894-1895
Marquess of Salisbury	1895-1902
Arthur Balfour	1902-1905
Sir H Campbell-Bannerman	1905-1908
Herbert Asquith	1908-1916
David Lloyd-George	1916-1922
Andrew Bonar Law	1922-1923
Stanley Baldwin	1923-1924
J Ramsay MacDonald	1924
Stanley Baldwin	1924-1929
J Ramsay MacDonald	1929-1935
Stanley Baldwin	1935-1937
Neville Chamberlain	1937-1940
Winston Churchill	1940-1945
Clement Attlee	1945-1951
Sir Winston Churchill	1951-1955
Sir Anthony Eden	1955-1957
Harold Macmillan	1957-1963
Sir Alec Douglas-Home	1963-1964
Harold Wilson	1964-1970
Edward Heath	1970-1974
Harold Wilson	1974-1976
James Callaghan	1976-1979
Margaret Thatcher	1979-1990
John Major	1990-1997
Tony Blair	1997-____

American Presidents

George Washington	1789-1797
John Adams	1797-1801
Thomas Jefferson	1801-1809
James Madison	1809-1817
James Monroe	1817-1825
John Quincy Adams	1825-1829
Andrew Jackson	1829-1837
Martin van Buren	1837-1841
William H Harrison	1841
John Tyler	1841-1845
James K Polk	1845-1849
Zachary Taylor	1849-1850
Millard Fillmore	1850-1853
Franklin Pierce	1853-1857
James Buchanan	1857-1861
Abraham Lincoln	1861-1865
Andrew Johnson	1865-1869
Ulysses S Grant	1869-1877
Rutherford B Hayes	1877-1881
James A Garfield	1881
Chester A Arthur	1881-1885
Grover Cleveland	1885-1889
Benjamin Harrison	1889-1893
Grover Cleveland	1893-1897
William McKinley	1897-1901
Theodore Roosevelt	1901-1909
William H Taft	1909-1913
Woodrow Wilson	1913-1921
Warren G Harding	1921-1923
Calvin Coolridge	1923-1929
Herbert C Hoover	1929-1933
Franklin D Roosevelt	1933-1945
Harry S Truman	1945-1953
Dwight D Eisenhower	1953-1961
John F Kennedy	1961-1963
Lyndon B Johnson	1963-1969
Richard M Nixon	1969-1974
Gerald R Ford	1974-1977
Jimmy Carter	1977-1981
Ronald Reagan	1981-1989
George Bush (Snr)	1989-1993
Bill Clinton	1993-2001
George Bush (Jnr)	2001-____

Bibliography and further reading

Airne, C W
The Story of Prehistoric and Roman Britain told in Pictures
Thomas Hope and Sankey Hudson Ltd

Atterbury, Paul
Victorians at Home and Abroad
V&A Publications (UK) 2001

Bender, Lionel
Eyewitness Guides: Inventions
Dorling Kindersley (UK) 1992

Bridgeman, Roger
Eyewitness Guides: Technology
Dorling Kindersley (UK) 1995

Clark, Paul and Freeman, Julian
Design, a Crash Course
The Ivy Press Ltd (UK) 2000

Cole, Alison
Eyewitness Guides: Renaissance
Dorling Kindersley (UK) 1994

Coote, Roger
The Anglo Saxons
Wayland (UK) 1993

Cox, Jane
London's East End, Life and Traditions
Weidefeld and Nicolson (UK) 1994

Davies, Gill
The Complete Stage Planning Kit
A & C Black UK 2003

Davies, Gill
Create Your Own Stage Effects
A & C Black (UK) 1999
Watson Guptill (USA) 1999

Davies, Gill
Create Your Own Stage Make-up
A & C Black (UK) 2001
Watson Guptill (USA) 2001

Davies, Gill
Create Your Own Stage Production
A & C Black (UK) 2000
Watson Guptill (USA) 2000

Davies, Gill
Staging a Pantomime
A & C Black (UK) 1995

Davies, Gill
Stage Source Book Sets
A & C Black (UK) 2004

Dick, Stewart and Allingham, Helen
The Cottage Homes of England
Bracken Books (UK) 1991

Fletcher, Banister
A History of Architecture
The Athlone Press (UK) 1961

Foote, P G and Wilson, D M
The Viking Achievement
Sidgwick and Jackson (UK) 1979

Forman, Joan
The Romans
Macdonald Educational (UK) 1975

Fry, Plantagenet Somerset
History of the World
Dorling Kindersley (UK) 1994

Gardiner, Juliet
From the Bomb to the Beatles
Collins and Brown (UK) 1999

Govier, Jacquie
Create Your Own Stage Props
A & C Black (UK) 1984
Prentice Hall Inc. (USA) 1984

Govier, Jacquie and Davies, Gill
Create Your Own Stage Costumes
A & C Black (UK), 1996
Heinemann. (USA) 1996

Hart, George
Eyewitness Guides: Ancient Egypt
Dorling Kindersley (UK) 1990

Haywood, John
The Romans
Oxford University Press (UK) 1994, 2001 (US) 1996

Higgins, Katherine
Collecting the 1970s
Miller's (UK) 2001

Houffe, Thomas
Design, a Concise History
Laurence King (UK) 1998

James, Simon
Eyewitness Guides: Ancient Rome
Dorling Kindersley (UK) 1990

Jenkins, J Geraint
Life and Tradition in Rural Wales
J M Dent and Sons (UK) 1976

Langley, Andrew
Eyewitness Guides: Medieval Life
Dorling Kindersley (UK) 1996

Lewis, June
The Cotswolds, Life and Traditions
Weidefeld and Nicolson (UK) 1996

Margeson, Susan
Eyewitness Guides: Viking
Dorling Kindersley (UK) 1994

Marsh, Madeleine
Collecting the 1960s
Miller's (UK) 1999

Massey, Anne
Interior Design of the 20th Century
Thomas and Hudson (UK) 2001

Matthews, Rupert
Eyewitness Guides: Explorer
Dorling Kindersley (UK) 1991

Murdoch, David
Eyewitness Guides: Cowboy
Dorling Kindersley (UK) 1993

Parsons, Martin
Air Raids: Britain at War
Wayland (UK) 1999

Pearson, Anne
Eyewitness Guides: Ancient Greece
Dorling Kindersley (UK) 1992

Penoyre, John and Ryan, Michael
The Observer's Book of Architecture
Frederick Warne (UK) 1975

Playne, Gill
The Timeline History of New York City
Palgrave Macmillan (USA) 2003
Worth Press Ltd (UK) 2003

Pragnerll, Hubert
The Styles of English Architecture
B T Batsford Ltd (UK) 1984

Porter, Valerie
Life Behind the Cottage Door
Whittet Books (UK) 1992

Reid, Richard
The Book of Buildings, a Traveller's Guide
Michael Joseph (UK) 1980

Sparke, Jenny
The Design Source Book
Macdonald (UK) 1986

Steele, Philio
House through the Ages
Eagle books

Thomas, Terry
Create Your Own Stage Sets
A & C Black (UK) 1985
Prentice Hall Inc. (USA) 1985
Watson Guptill (USA) 1999

Tubb, Jonathan
Bible Lands
Dorling Kindersley (UK) 1991

Wood, Richard
Bedrooms Through the Ages
Wayland (UK) 1999

Wright, Michael (Editor)
Treasures in Your Home
Reader's Digest Assoc. (UK) 1993

Twentieth Century Design series:
Jones, Helen
'40s and '50s: War and Post-War Years

Bingham, Julia
'60s: The Plastic Age

Gaff, Jackie
'70s and '80s: The High-Tech Age
and
1900-1920: The Birth of Modernism

Ford, Hannah
The '90s: The Digital Age
Heinemann Library (UK) 1999

Index

10 Downing Street 78
42nd Street 132
84 Charing Cross Road 146

A

Abelard and Heloise 36
Abu Simbel 11
Absurd Person Singular 94
Abydos 9
Acropolis 16
Actors 16
Addinsell, R 104
Aeroplanes 97, 101
Aeschylus 16
Admiral Chrichton, the 110
Africa 122-23
Afterlife 9
Aghia Sofia 31
Agincourt 143
Agnew, FEM
Agora 16
Ahmose 10
Aida 9
Akhenaten 14
Aladdin 120
Albee, Edward 94, 95
Alchemist, The 53, 95
Alexander the Great 10, 17, 23
Alexandria 10
Alfie 94
Alfred the Great 28, 30
Alice through the Looking Glass 104, 112
Allen, J P 94
Amadeus 64, 66
America 30, 98, 132
American Buffalo 146
American War of Independence 74
Ampitheatres 16, 22
Ancient Egypt 8-14, 95
Ancient Greece 15-20, 136
Ancient Rome 21-27
Amundsen 83
Andersen, Hans C 126, 150
Anglo-Saxon 29, 30
An Inspector Calls 94
Anastasia 94
Anna Karenina 126, 144
Annie Get your Gun 140
Anouilh, Jean 36
Anthony and Cleopatra 9, 22
Antique shop 146
Aqueducts 23, 24, 27
Arabs 10, 30
Arch of Septimus Severus 26

Archimedes 23
Arenas 16
Aristophanies 16
Armada, Spanish 44
Arsenic and Old Lace 94
Art Nouveau 83, 95
Artemis 19
Arts and Crafts 83, 86, 95
Arthur, King 30
Arycanda 24
Ashley, Laura 95
Asia Minor 17
Assyrian 10, 17
Astronomers 15, 54
Aswan 10
Atahualpa 44
Athenians 17
Athens 16, 18, 19
Auditoriums 42
Austen, Jane 42, 82
Australia 125
Ayers Rock 125
Ayckbourn, Alan 94, 95, 106, 108, 112, 144

B

Babes in the Wood 104
Baboon 14
Bacchae, The 16
Bakehouse 97 Ballet 100, 150
Barbarian 29
Barber of Seville 136
Barber's shop 146
Barefoot in the Park 132
Barnum 82, 142
Baroque 60
Baroness Orczy 128
Barrie, J M 104, 110
Bart, Lionel 66, 130
Bartholomew Fair 53, 142
Basil 30
Bath 78
Baths and bathrooms 22
Bauhaus 95
Baum, L Frank 148
Beach 110
Beaufoy, Simon 95
Beauty and the Beast 148
Beaux Stratagem, the 64
Becket 36
Bedrooms 58-59, 69, 98, 100
Beds 49. 58-59, 72
Beggar's Opera, the 66
Bells 9
Benatzky, Ralph 115
Ben Hur 22
Bennett, Alan 66

Bennett, M 132
Bont Pyramid 9
Berlin, Irving 140
Bernstein, L 94, 132
Beverly Cross 146
Bible 54
Billy Liar 94
Bizet 136
Black Death 35, 37
Blackmore, R D 53, 106, 108
Bleasdale, Alan
Blue Remembered Hills 94, 106
Bodleian Library 60
Bogdanov, Michael 140
Boleyn, Anne 49
Bolt, Robert 43, 130
Bond, Edward 110
Book of Kells, the 32
Bookshop 146
Boot shop 146
Bottom's Dream 43
Boublil 95, 120
Bow Bridge 62
Boy with a Cart 29
Boyfriend, The 94
Bramble, M 82, 132, 142
Brand, Max 140
Brecht, Bertolt 22, 120, 124, 126, 136, 143
Breton chateau 51
Brideshead Revisited 112
Bridges 50, 57, 700
Briggs, Raymond 150
Brighouse, Harold 146
Britain 23, 29
British Museum 84, 95
Britannicus 22
Britons 30
Brontë, Charlotte 82
Brontë, Emily 106
Brownstone terraces 133
Buckingham Palace 86
Building 9
Burial 10
Burrows, Abe 82, 132, 138
Burton, B J 82, 106, 130
Byzantine 10, 30, 37, 39

C

Cabaret 94
Caesar and Cleopatra 9
Caesarea 23
Cairo 10
Calamity Jane 140
Caliph 10
Caliph Omar 31
Camelot 29, 35, 36
Camille 82
Can Can 75, 82
Canephora 19
Cannon 49
Canterbury Tales 36

Capital 13, 19, 27, 50
Capitol, Virginia 80
Cardinal Wolsley 46
Carmen 136
Carolean 57
Carousel 142
Carriage 69
Carroll, Lewis 104
Cars 97, 99, 102
Caryatid 19
Casey 94
Castles 36, 50
Cathedrals 39, 41, 63, 101
Cause Célèbre 94
Cavalier 52
Ceasar & Cleopatra 9, 22
Ceasar 23
Celtic 33, 34
Celtic Britons 29, 32
Celtic cross 32
Celts 17
Central Park 132-133
Chambers, John 29
Charlemagne 30
Charles I 54
Charles II 54
Charles V 44
Charley's Aunt 82
Charlton House 60
Chateau 51, 71
Chaucer 36
Chekhov 82, 112
Cherry Orchard, The 82
Children 54
Chimneys 46, 49
China 37
China, Great Wall of 23
Chinese 30, 79
Chorus Line, A 95
Chorus of Disapproval, A 95
Chorus Line, A 94, 132
Christ 23
Christianity 21, 22, 23, 28, 29
Christie, Agatha 9, 122, 144
Christmas Carol, A 82
Chrysler Building 132
Chu Chin Chow 120
Churches 29, 32, 39, 40, 43
Cider with Rosie 106
Cinderella 148
Circus 82, 142
Circus Maximum 22
Cities 22
Civil war 54
Civilisation 16
Cladius 23
Clarinets 9
Cleopatra 10
Clifford, J 134
Clink, The 43
Clocks 73, 99
Clouds 117
Coach 73

Coffins and tombs 9
Coke, Peter 146
Cold Comfort Farm 112
Coleman, Cy 82, 142
Coleshill 58
Colette 94, 128
Collins, W 82
Colosseum 22, 23, 24
Colossoi of Memnon 11
Columns 12, 13, 18-19, 26, 50
Comédie Française 53
Computers 94, 96
Confectionery 146
Congreve, William 66
Conquest 35, 37, 38
Constantine 23, 31
Constantinople 10, 23, 30
Copernicus 42, 44
Coppel, Alec 112
Copper 9
Cora 27
Corinthian 17, 19, 23, 26, 27
Coriolanus 22
Cortes 42, 44
Cottages 68-69, 87
Couch 73
Count Dracula 78
Country 44
Country house 89
Country Wife 53
Courtyards 16
Covent Garden 146
Covered bridge 61
Coward, Noel 94, 136
Cracks 95
Crime 54
Cromwell 53, 54
Cromwellian 58
Cross, B 128
Crown Matrimonial 94, 130
Crucible, the 53
Crusades 35, 37
Curtmantle 36
Cyclorama 117
Cymbals 9
Cyrano de Bergerac 53

D

Da Vinci, Leonardo 37, 42
Dahshur 9
Daisy Pulls it Off 94
Dale, Jim 136
Dame of Sark, the
Danegeld 28
Danelaw 30
Dane, C 104
Danes 28, 29, 30, 34
Dante 94, 132
Dark Ages, The 28-34
Daviot, Gordon 36

De Marne, Denis 130
Dear Brutus 104
Death of a Salesman 94
Death in Venice 134
Death on the Nile 9
Decorated 41
Decoration 9
Deegan, Denise 94
Delaney, Shelagh 94
Delpi 18
Denmark 126
Desert Song 122
Destry Rides Again 140
Devils, the 53
Dewhurst, Keith 82, 106
Diary of Anne Frank 94, 126
Dick Whittington 130, 148
Dickens, Charles 66, 82, 87, 128, 130
Dickensian 130
Dionysus 16
Disappeared 132
Disney 148
Doctors 15
Dome of the Rock 31
Domestic interiors 62
Don't Look Now 134
Dona Rosita the Spinster or the Language of Flowers 136
Doors 39, 50, 76-78, 84
Doric 17, 19, 27
Double pipes 9
Downing, Street 78
Doyle, Sir A C 82, 106
Draco 17
Drake 42, 44
Draper's shop 146
Dressers 69
Dressing table 73, 91
Drums 9
Drunkard, the or Down with Demon Drink! 130
Dry goods store 146
Du Maurier 134
Dubin, A 132
Duchess of Malfi, the 53
Duffy, C A 148
Dumas 53, 128
Dungeons 36
Dunlop, Frank 136
Dynasties 9
Dynasty, First 9
Dynasty, Fourth 9, 10
Dynasty, Han 23
Dynasty, Second 9
Dynasty, Third 9

E

Early English 40

Index

Early Victorian 84
East Anglia 29
East India Company 54
Easter 29
Edfu 13
Edmund 132
Edward VI 44
Edward the Elder 30
Edwardian 36
Egypt 8-12, 17, 30
Egypt, Lower 10
Egypt, Upper 10
Egyptians 8-14
Eiffel Tower 128
Elizabeth I 42, 44, 49
Elizabethan 44-49, 59
Emperor 23, 30
Empire 21, 22, 23, 29, 30, 37
Empire State Building 132-133
England 28, 30, 34, 36, 37, 42, 44, 53, 54
Entertainment 54
Ephesus 26
Erechtheion 19
Eric the Red 30
Esna 13
Ethelred, King 28
Euclid 17
Euripides 16
European Baroque 60
European Renaissance 50-51
Executive homes 101
Exteriors 103-118

F

Fain, Sammy 140
Fairgrounds 142
Fairy tale 148-9
Fall 112
Famine 9
Far East 120-121
Far from the Madding Crowd 106
Farmhouses 45, 55, 57, 59, 68-69
Farquhar, George 66
Feydeau, George 94
Field 106-107
Fielding 66
Fields H & D 140
Fire escape 133
Fire of London 53-4, 62-3
Fireplaces 39, 50, 54, 74
Firstborn 9
Firth & Forth bridge 98
Firth, Tim 108
Flags 80, 90
Flatiron Building 133
Flea in her Ear, a 94
Flower Drum Song 120
Flutes 9
Follow that Girl 130
Fontainebleau 60

Ford, John 53
Forest 104-105, 148
Forts 23
Fortuna Virilis, Temple of 27
Forum 22, 26
Four-poster bed 49, 58, 68
France 39, 44, 136
Francis 36
Francis, Matthew 128
Frankenstein 82
Fraser-Simson 148
Freeman, CK 140
French palaces 61
French Revolution 66, 67
French without Tears 136
Front Page, The 58
Fry, Christopher 9, 16, 29, 36, 53, 108
Fry, Michael 106
Full Monty, the 95
Funny Thing Happened on the Way to the Forum, a 22
Furnishings 9, 23, 43, 66

G

Galileo 42, 54
Galleon 49
Gaminara, William 126
Gardens 48, 49, 112-114
Gardner, Herb 132
Gaslight 78
Gates 70, 77
Gaul 23
Gelbart, Larry 22
Gay, John 66
Gazebo, the 112
Gems, Pam 82
Genghis Khan 37
Geometry in Venice 134
German townhall 51
Germinal 126
Gershe, Leonard 140
Gibbons, Sheila 112
Ghost Train, the 144
Gigi 94, 128
Gilbert & Sullivan 82, 120, 130, 134
Giza 10
Gladiator 22, 24
Globe, the 43, 53, 63, 71
Godber, John 136
Gods 9, 13, 17
Gogol 78
Gold 9, 10, 54
Golden Gate Bridge 98
Goldilocks 104
Goldman, James 36
Goldsmith, Oliver 66

Gondoliers, the 134
Goodbye Iphigenia 16
Goodrich, Frances 94, 126
Gothic 39, 43, 53, 56
Goths 29
Götterdämmerung 29
Government Inspector, The 78
Grahame, K 108, 148
Grand Central 132, 144
Grand or great houses 47, 70-71
Grapes Inn 87
Gray, Nicholas Stuart 120
Grease 94
Great Expectations 82
Great Pyramid 10
Great Waltz, the
Greece 15, 16, 17, 18, 136
Greeks 15-20
Green, George M 16
Greenland 30
Greenwood, D 136
Grimm Tales 148
Groseti 14
Grun, Bernard 115
Guggenheim Museum 133
Guillotine 67 ?
Gunpowder 54
Gupta 23
Guys and Dolls 132, 138
Gypsy's Revenge, the 104

H

Hackett, Albert 84, 126
Hadrian's Wall 23
Hair 94
Half a Sixpence 146
Hall, Willis 53, 82, 94, 108, 124, 128, 143
Hamilton, Patrick 82
Hamlisch, M 9, 94, 132
Hammerstein, Oscar 108
Hamp 143
Hampton, C 66
Hampton Court 48
Han Dynasty 23
Hanff, Helene 146
Hansel and Gretel 104
Hard God, A 125
Harding, Mike 143
Hardy, Thomas 106
Harp 9
Hart, Moss 144
Harwood, Ronald 146
Hathor 10
Hatshepsut 10
Health 67
Hearth 48. 56
Hedda Gabler 82
Heidelberg Castle 50

Heidi 115
Heiress, the 82
Hellenic 17
Hellenistic 17
Heneker, David 146
Henry V 36, 143
Henry VII 43, 44
Henry VIII 43, 130
Hiawatha 140
Hibbert, Guy 138
Hieroglyphic 10
High Profiles 130
Highwaymen 54
Hill, Ken 122
Hippocrates 17
Hippocratic Oath 17
Hobson's Choice 146
Holman, David 150
Homecoming, The 94
Homes 22, 30, 53, 66, 85, 97-101
Honington Hall 59
Honour of God, The 36
Hood, Robin 36
Hotels 100
Hound of the Baskervilles, the 82
House of Mirth, the 144
Houses of Parliament 86
Hunchback of Notre Dame 128
Hugo, V 128
Hundred Year War 37
Huns Ibis 14
Hyem, Jill 53, 106, 108

I

Ibis 14
Ibsen, Henrik 82, 122, 126
Ice 150
I'm not Rappaport 132
Imperial Nightingale 120
Importance of Being Earnest, the 82
Incas 37, 44
India 17, 124
Indian Ink 124
Infirmary 89
International guidelines 119-138
Iolanthe 78, 130
Ionian 26
Ionic 17, 19, 26
Iran 17
Ireland 28, 29, 32
Island, The 110
Israel 23
Istanbul 31
Italian Renaissance 136
Italy 136, 161
Ivan The Terrible 42, 44

J

Jack and the Beanstalk 148
Jack and the Baked Bean Stalk 125
Jack the Ripper 130
Jacobean 52-56, 62
Jacobs 94
James I 53, 54, 61
James II 54
James, Henry 82
Jane Eyre 82
Japan 17, 30, 44
Jeffreys, Stephen 4, 53
Jellicoe, Ann 94
Jerusulem 31, 37
Joan of Arc 37
John, Elton 9
Jones, Inigo 53, 61
Jones, Marie 110
Jonson, Ben 53, 142
Joseph and His Amazing Technicolour Dreamcoat 9
Journey's End 94, 143
Jousting 38
Julius Caesar 22
June Moon 132
Jungle 124, 138
Jungle Book 124
Junk shop 146
Juno and the Paycock 94
Justinian 30, 31

K

Kadesh 10
Kander and Ebb 94
Karnak 10
Kaufman, G S 132, 144
Keeler Dawn 132, 144
Kelly, Tim 82, 106
Keneally, Thomas 125
Kenna, Peter 12
Kesselring, Joseph 94
Khafre 10
King and I, the
King Ethelred 28
King of Wessex 30
Kingdom of Franks 30
Kings 9, 10
Kingsley, Charles 108
Kipps 146
Kipling, Rudyard 124
Kirkwood 94, 132
Kitchens 69, 95, 98, 100, 101
Kleban E 94, 132
Knack, The 94
Kyoto 30

L

Lady Audley's Secret 82
Lady's not for Burning 36
Lakeland 108-109
Lakes 150
Lambe, Michael 104
Lardner, R 132
Lark 36
Lark Rise 82, 106
Late Victorian 86
Laura Ashley 96
Laurents, Arthur 132
Le Bourgeois Gentilhomme 128
Le Corbusier 97
Lebanon 9
Lee , Laurie 106
Leonard, Hugh 82, 136
Lerner, A J 29, 36, 94, 146
Les Liasons Dangereuses 66
Levy, Benn W 16
Lewis, C S 104, 148, 150
Libertine, the 53
Library 97
Libyans 10
Life at home 16
Life of Galileo, the 136
Lifestyle 9, 29, 66, 79, 95, 96
Lightning 118
Lillo, George 64
Linnebach 82
Lion in Winter, the 36
Lion, the Witch and the Wardrobe, the 104, 148, 150
Little Mermaid, the 126
Little Red Riding Hood 132, 148
Living rooms 97, 99, 100
Lloyd Webber, Andrew 9
Lock up Your Daughters 66
Loesser, Frank 132, 138
Loewe, F 29, 36, 94, 146
London 82, 84, 86, 87, 130
London Merchant, the 64
Long and the Short and the Tall, the 94, 124
Long March, the 143
Longhouse 33
Lonsdale, Frederick 115
Lorca, FG 136
Lorna Doone 53, 106, 108
Losing Venice 134

Index

Lotus Flower 14
Louis XIV 53, 54
Louvre Pyramid 100, 129
Love of the Nightingale 16
Lutes 9
Luther 43
Luxor 11
Lyres 9, 16
Lysistrata 16

M

Macalpine, J 66
Macedon, Philip II 17
Macedonia 23
Macedonian Dynasty 30
MacDermot 94
MacDonald, S 110, 143
MacEwan Green, G 16
MacKenzie, M 134
Madame Butterfly 120
Made in Bangkok 120
Madness of George III 66
Magellan 42
Magistrate, the 82
Magna Carta 37
Maid of the Mountains 115
Mally 95, 120
Man for All Seasons, a 43, 130
Man is Man (Man equals Man) 124
Mandel, Frank 122
Manet, David 132
Manhattan Island 132
Manor houses 36
Mansfield Park 82
Mansion House 78
Mansions 56, 66, 92
Mantelpieces 39, 70-71
Mann, Thomas 134
Map of the Heart 122
Marco Polo 37
Markets 60, 146
Mamey, David 146
Marriage 54
Martin, Steve 128
Mary 54
Mary, Queen of Scots 44
Mary Stuart 43
Masks 16, 22
Massinger, Philip 22
Mastaba 10
Matchgirls, the 82
Maurette, Marcelle 94
Mayan 30
Mayflower 54
McGuinness, Frank 143
Meadow 106-107
Medea 16
Medicine 67

Medina 30
Medinet Habu 13
Mediterranean 16, 136
Melodrama 144
Memkure 10
Memnon, Colossus of 11
Memphis 9
Menander 16
Merchant of Venice, the 134
Metropolitan Museum 133
Mentuhotep II 10
Mesopotamia 17
Mexico 44 138
Middle Ages, the 35-41
Middle Kingdom 10, 14
Midsummer's Night Dream, a 104
Mikado 120
Miles, Bernard 66
Milestone 87, 149
Military 143
Millar, Ronald 36
Millennium Eye 130
Miller, Arthur 53, 94
Milne, A A 106, 108, 148
Mind if I Sit Here 125
Ming Dynasty 54
Minghella, Anthony 36, 120
Mirrors 74
Misanthrope, The 53
Miser, the 128
Miss Saigon 95, 120
Mitchell, Julian 36
Mobile home 101
Mohammed 30
Molière 53, 128
Monasteries 28, 29
Mongol 37
Month in the Country, a 82
Moon 118
Morecombe and Wise
Morley, John 108
Morris, William 86
Mosaics 17, 24
Moscow Stations 144
Motorbike 101
Mother, the 126
Mother Courage and her Children 143
Mountains 115, 116, 138, 150
Mulrine, Stephen 144
Mummies 10
Mummy's Tomb, the 122
Murder of Maria Marten 82, 106
Murder on the Nile 122
Murder on the Orient Express 144
Music hall 94
Muslims 30, 37

My Fair Lady 94, 146
Myths 9

N

Nagy, Phyllis 132
Nana 128
Napolean I 60
Narmer 10
Nash, John 84
National Gallery 84
Native American 140
Nativity 29
Naughton, Bill 94
Nesbit, E 144
Neville's Island 108
New Amsterdam 132
New Kingdom 10
Newton 54, 71
New England 57
New World 37
New York 132
Nichols, Peter 124, 143
Nicholson, W 94, 122
Night and Day 122
Night of the Iguana 94, 138
Night Must Fall 94
Nicol, Ron 150
Nile 9, 10
Nomadic 10
Norman 30, 35, 37-39, 40
Northern Europe 126
Norton, Frederick 120
Northumberland 29
Not about Heroes 143
Not with a Bang 143
Notre Dame 39
Nubia 9, 10
Nubians 10
Nunsense II: the Second Coming 137
Nutcracker Suite 150

O

O'Casey, Sean 94
Obelisk 8
Oboes 9
Observe the Sons of Ulster Marching towards the Somme 143
Oedipus at Colonus 16
Oedipus the King 16
Offices 101
Ogham Stone 32
Oh, What a Lovely War! 143
Oklahoma 140
Old Kingdom 9, 10
Oliver 130
Olympiad 17
Omas, Caliph 31
On the Razzle 128
Once in a Lifetime 144

Orchestra 16
Orient 120-121, 148
Orlean 37
Ornate styles 73
Orpheus Descending 146
Osborne, John 43, 82, 94
Osiris 13
Osment, Philip
Otto I 30
Ottoman Empire 37
Our Country's Good 125
Owen, Bill 82

P

Pageant 9
Paintings, wall 13
Palace of Westminster 86
Palaces 9, 64, 70
Palm 13
Pantheon 27
Pantomime 110, 142
Papyrus 13, 14
Paris 39, 54, 100, 102, 128
Paris Opera 78
Parkes, D 136
Parsley, Roger 112
Parthenon 18
Parthenon 23, 27
Passion Killers 136
Patrick, Saint 28
Peer Gynt 82, 122, 126
Peloponnesian 17
Pember, Ron 130
Pentelic 17
Perpendicular 39, 41
Persians 10, 17, 30
Peru 37
Peter and the Wolf 148
Peter Pan 110
Peter Rabbit 106
Peter the Great 54
Pharoahs 8, 9, 10
Philae 13
Philosophers 15
Phoenix too Frequent, a 16
Pi 10
Piano 16
Picasso at the Lapin Agile 128
Pied Piper 148
Pillars 13
Pinero 78
Pinocchio 142
Pinter 94
Pitt, G D 82
Pizarro 44
Plague 52, 54, 62
Plautus 22
Plaza Suite 132
Plough and the Stars 94

Poets 15
Poliakoff, Stephen
Pompei 23
Pompeius 22, 24
Pope Gregory 30
Poole, Alan 43
Porter, Cole 82
Portraits 71
Ports 23
Portugal 136
Posford, George 115
Potter, Beatrix 106
Potter, Dennis 94, 106, 136
Pre-fab 98
Presson Allen, Jay 94
Priestley, J B 94
Prime of Miss Jean Brodie, The 94
Prior, Judith 125
Private Lives 94, 136
Privates on Parade 124, 143
Prodigious Snob, The 128
Prokofiev 148
Promenade 110
Ptolemy II 10
Pubs 87
Puccini 120
Punic Wars 23
Puritan 52-53
Puss in Boots 148
Pygmalion 146
Pyramid, Bent 9
Pyramids 8-11
Pythagoras 17

Q

Queen 10
Queen Mary I 44
Queen of Scots, Mary 44
Queen's House, Greenwich 57

R

Racine 22, 53
Rado 94
Ragni 94
Railway 144
Railway Children, the 144
Raleigh, Sir Walter 45
Ramsesses II 10
Rape of the Belt 16
Rattigan, Terence 94, 136
Rattles 9
Real Thing, The
Recruiting Officer, the 66
Red Riding Hood 104
Red House, Kent 86
Regency 82, 94-95

Renaissance 36, 42, 44, 45, 50, 56
Renolds and Slade 130
Restoration 53
Rhinegold, The 29
Rice, Tim 9
Ridley, Arnold 144
Rice, Tim 9
Richard III 36, 143
Richard of Bordeaux 36
Rimco, L 9
Rivals, the 66
Rivers 108-109
Roads 23
Roaring Twenties 94
Roasting spit
Robin Hood 36, 104
Robbins, G 148
Robbins, Jerome 94
Robbins, Norman
Robin Hood 94
Robinson Crusoe 110
Rock of the Dome 31
Rodgers & Hammerstein 94, 115, 120
Roman times 136
Romanesque 39, 40
Romantic Movement 78
Romanov Dynasty 54
Romans 10, 17, 21-27, 28, 29, 30, 42, 44
Roman Actor, the 22
Roman Fever 136
Romberg Sigmund 122
Rome 17, 19, 21-27, 30, 44, 136
Rome, Harold 140
Rookery Nook 94
Roose-Evans, J 146
Rosencrantz and Guildenstern are Dead 43
Roses of Eyam 53
Ross 94, 122
Rossini 136
Rostrand, Edmund 53
Round and Round the Garden 112
Royal Hospital 61
Royal Hunt of the Sun, the 43, 138
Royal Pavilion, Brighton 84
Royalty 9
Ryton, Royce 94, 130
Runestones 31
Russell, Tony 82
Russell, Willy 110, 136
Russia 30, 42, 44
Ryton, Royce 94

S

Saint George 36
St James Palace 48

Index

St Mark's, Venice 39
Saint Patrick 28
St Paul's Cathedral 53, 63
St Peter's Hospital 60
Sanakht 9
Saqqara 9, 10
Sarcophagus 10
Sassoon, Vidal
Satires 9
Saturn, Temple of 26
Saunders, James 110, 112
Savages
Saxon 29, 30, 40
Scandinavia 126
Scapino 136
Scarab beetle 14
Scarlet Pimpernel, The 66, 128
Schiller, Friedrich 43
School for Scandal 66
Schonberg 95, 120
Science 54
Scientists 15
Scotland 28
Sea, The 110
Seagull, The 82
Seaside 110-111
Semi-detached 98
Seneca 22
Seven Wonders 10
Shadowlands 94
Shaffer, Peter 43, 66, 138
Shakespeare, William 9, 16, 22, 36, 42, 43, 53, 104, 110, 130, 134, 143
Shaw, George B 9, 22, 94, 146
Shelley, Mary 82
She Stoops to Conquer 66
Sheridan 66
Sheriff, R C 94, 143
Sherman 95
Shevelove, Burt 22
Shirley Valentine 110, 136
Shops and shopping 22, 37, 90, 97 100, 101, 146
Shore 110-111
Shoredtch 62
Shotoku, Prince 30
Showboat 108
Sicily 17
Siegfried 29
Simon, Neil 132
Slaves 9, 44
Simpson, Dave 144
Sisterly Feelings 106
Sky 117-118
Skyscraper 102, 133
Sleeping Beauty 104, 148
Slums 83, 85
Snefru, King 9
Socrates 17

Sondheim, Stephen 22
Snow 150
Snow Queen, the 150
Snowman, the 150
Snow White and the Seven Dwarfs 148
Sofa 73
Sondheim Stephen 132
Sophocles 16
Sound of Music, the
South America 138
Southern Europe 136
Space rocket 102
Spain 23, 30, 36, 136
Spanish Armada 44
Spanish Inquisition 37
Sparta 17
Sphinx 10, 11
Spinning wheel 55
Spyri, Johanna 115
Staircases 71, 73
Stars 118
State of Revolution
Statesmen 15
Stations 144
Statue of Liberty 91, 132
Step Pyramid 9, 10
Stevenson, R L 82
Stoker, Bram 82
Stone buildings 46
Stoppard, Tom 43, 122, 124, 126
Strangeness of Others, the 130
Stream 108-109
Street scene 38, 146
Stewart 82
Stuart, M 132
Stuart style 57
Surbubia 87
Sufficient Carbohydrate 136
Sullivan, G 128
Supermarket 95, 101
Supple, T 148
Surprise Package 136
Swan Lake 108
Sweeney Todd 82, 146
Sydney Opera House 125

T

T'ang Dynasty 30
Taj Mahal 54
Taking Sides
Tale of Two Cities, a 66, 128
Talented Mr Ripley, the
Tales of King Arthur 29
Tambourines 9
Tartar 23
Taste of Honey, a 94
Taylor, Don 53
Tchaikovsky 108, 150
Television 95, 99, 100
Tell el-Amarna 14
Tempest, the 53

Temple of Fortuna Virilis 27
Temple of Saturn 26
Temples 9, 10, 12, 16, 18-19, 23, 26
Tenements 132
Terence 22
Terraced row 83, 87, 88
Tess of the d'Ubervilles 106
Theatre, Victorian 88
Theatre Workshop Chilton, C 143
Theatres, Greek 20
Theatres, Roman 24
Thebes 13
Thespis 16
Thirty Year War 54
This Happy Breed 94
Thomas, Brandon 82
Thomas, Dylan 94, 110
Thompson, Flora 82, 106
Thor, With Angels 29
Thoth 14
Three Musketeers, the 53, 128
Three Tall Women 95
Throne 38
Tiffany 98
Tilting Ground 138
Timber frame 45
Times Square 132
Tis Pity She's A Whore 53
Toad of Toad Hall 148
Tolstoy 126, 144
Tomalin, Claire 144
Tombs 8, 9, 10, 17
Tom Jones 66
Tomb with a View
Tower of London 38, 49, 130
Town Hall 51
Town house 89
Towns 22, 37, 44
Trafalgar Square 82
Tragedy 16
Trains 144
Travers, Ben 94
Treasure Island 82, 110
Trees 150
Trelawny of the 'Wells' 82
Trial of Lucullus 22
Trinity College 59
Troilus and Cressida 16
Troja Palace 60
Trojan Women, the 16
Trumpets 9
Tudor 35, 37, 42, 43, 45, 46, 47
Tudor rose 49
Turandot 120
Turgenev 82
Turkey 24, 26
Turn of the Screw, the 82
Tutankhamun 10

Twin Towers 100
Two planks and a passion 36

U

Ugly Duckling 108
Under Milk Wood 94, 110
Urns 68
USA 62, 80, 90-92, 97, 98, 132-33
Utility furniture 95, 98

V

Valkyrie, The 29
Valley of Echoes 115
Valley of the Kings 10
Vance, Charles 106
Vandals 29
Van Trapp 115
Venice 39, 134
Venus Observed 108
Verdi 9
Versailles 60, 61
Vespasian 24
Vespucci 44
Vesuvius 23
Victoria, Queen 86
Victorian 84, 86, 87, 89
Vietnam war 106, 110, 111
Viking dancing god 33
Viking impact 30
Vikings 28-34
Virginia 74
Vivat! Vivat! Regina 43
Volkswagen 95, 99
Volute 13

W

Wagner, Richard 29, 75, 82
Wales 28, 29
Walker 138
Wallace, JT 128
Wall painting 13, 14
Wall, Hadrian's 23
Wand 132
War 81, 83, 88, 90, 143
Ward, N 132
Wardrobe 80, 93
Warhol, Andy 105, 110
War of the Roses 37, 45
Warren, H 132
Wars of the Roses 143
Washing machine 96
Washington 90
Washstand 96
Water Babies, The 108
Waterhouse, K 94
Watling Street 30
Waugh, Evelyn 112
Way, Brian 115

Way of the World, the 66
Way Upstream 95, 108
Webster, John 53
Webster, PF 140
Wells, H.G. 146
Wertenbaker, Timberlake 16, 125
Westover House 80
West Side Story 94, 132
Westonbirt School 84
Westminster 130
Westerns 138
Whale 150
Wharton Edith 132, 136, 144
What Are Little Girls Made Of? 146
When I was a Girl I used to Scream and Shout 110
When We Are Married 94
White Horse Inn 115
White House 91
White, Matthew 106
White Tower 38
Whitehall 53
Whiting, John 53
Who's Afraid of Virginia Woolf? 95
Why Not Stay for Breakfast
Wild West 140, 144
Wilde, Oscar 82, 112
William 54
Williams, Emlyn 82, 94
Williams, Paula 125
Williams, Tennessee 94, 138, 146
Wilson, John 143
Wilson, Sandy 94
Wind of Heaven, the 82
Wind in the Willows 108
Windows 76
Winnie the Pooh 106
Winslow Boy, the 94
Winter Guest 110
Winter Wife, the 144
Wizard of Oz 148
Wolsely, Cardinal 46
Woman in White 82
Women on the edge of HRT 110
Woodland 104-105
Word from our Sponsor, A 144
Work 54
Workers Institute 97
World War I 143
World War II 63, 95, 143
Wren, Christopher 61-63
Wuthering Heights 106

Wyatt, Woodrow 130
Wycherley, William 53
Wymark, O 128

Y

York Watergate 61

Z

Zeughaus Danzig 60
Zeus 19
Zola, Emile 126, 128
Zoser 9